Best Editorial Cartoons of the Year

DAVID HORSEY
Courtesy Seattle Post-Intelligencer

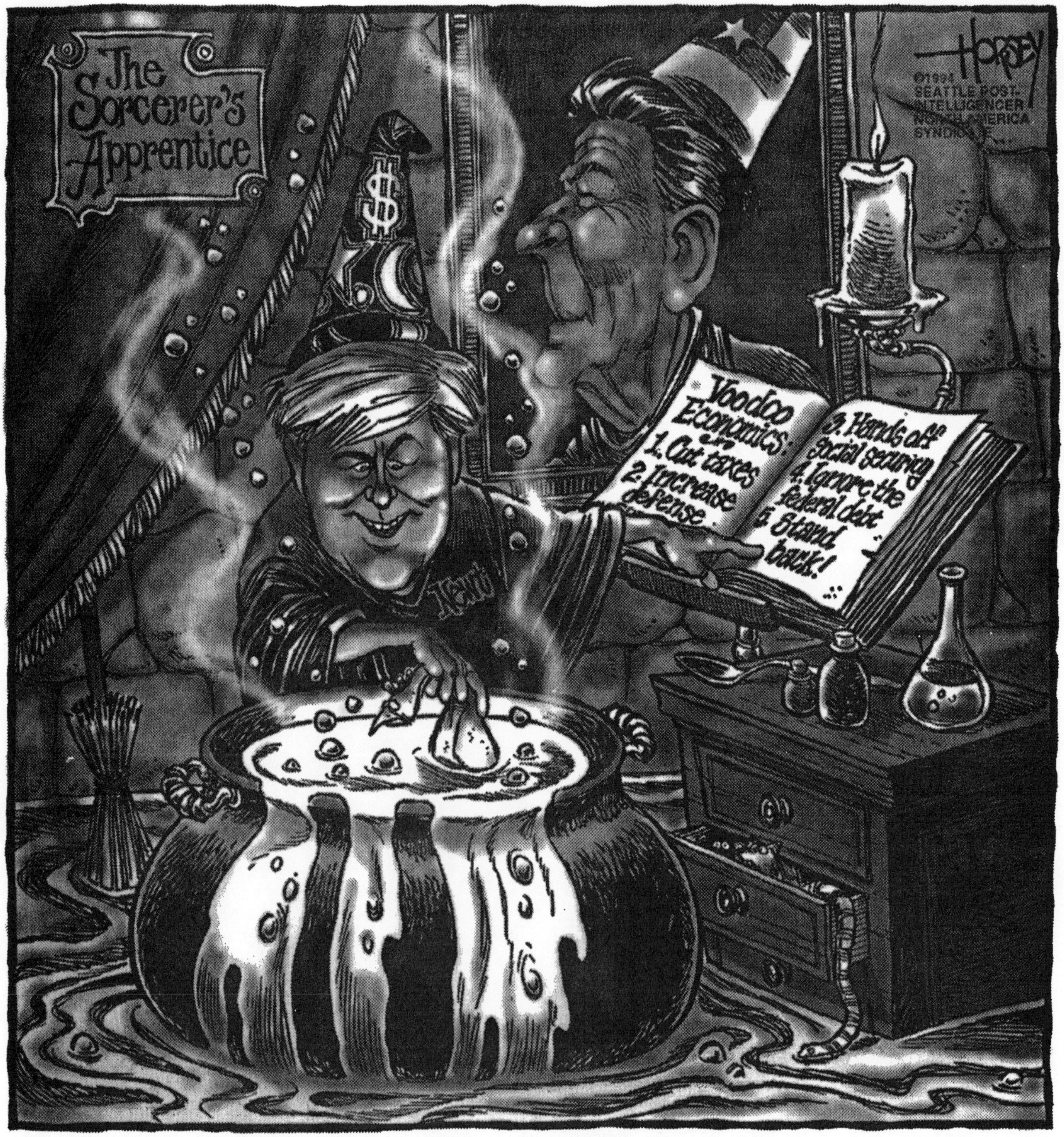
The Sorcerer's Apprentice
HORSEY
©1994 SEATTLE POST-INTELLIGENCER NORTH AMERICA SYNDICATE
$
Voodoo Economics:
1. Cut taxes
2. Increase defense
3. Hands off Social security
4. Ignore the federal debt
5. Stand back!
Newt

BEST EDITORIAL CARTOONS OF THE YEAR

1995 EDITION

Edited by
CHARLES BROOKS

PELICAN PUBLISHING COMPANY
Gretna 1995

Library of Congress Serial Catalog Data

Best editorial cartoons. 1972-
    Gretna [La.] Pelican Pub. Co.
    v. 29 cm annual-
"A pictorial history of the year."

    1. United States—Politics and government—
1969—Caricatures and Cartoons—Periodicals.
E839.5.B45   320.9'7309240207   73-643645
ISSN 0091-2220   MARC-S

Manufactured in the United States of America
Published by Pelican Publishing Company, Inc.
1101 Monroe Street, Gretna, Louisiana 70053

Contents

Award-Winning Cartoons

1994 PULITZER PRIZE

MICHAEL RAMIREZ
Editorial Cartoonist
Memphis Commercial Appeal

Born in Tokyo, Japan; graduate of the University of California at Irvine; editorial cartoonist for the *Newport Ensign* and the *Daily Sun* and *Post*, San Clemente, California; syndicated by Copley News Service, 1986 to the present; cartoonist for the *Memphis Commercial Appeal*, 1990 to the present; cartoons syndicated to 950 newspapers, including *USA Today*.

YOU HAVE TO EXPECT SOME CUTBACKS WITH THE CLINTON HEALTH PLAN...

MIKE PETERS
Editorial Cartoonist
Dayton Daily News

Native of St. Louis, Missouri; graduate of Washington University, 1965; editorial cartoonist for the *Chicago Daily News,* 1965-69, and the *Dayton Daily News,* 1969 to the present; winner of the Pulitzer Prize for Cartooning, 1981, the National Headliners Club Award, 1982 and 1987, the National Society of Professional Journalists Award, 1985, and the Reuben Award, 1992.

1994 FISCHETTI AWARD

JOHN DEERING
Editorial Cartoonist
Arkansas Democrat-Gazette

Born in Little Rock, Arkansas, 1956; studied art at the University of
Arkansas at Little Rock; sculptor of the Arkansas Vietnam Veterans
Memorial; awarded the Distinguished Service Medal for the memorial
sculpture, 1990; winner of seven first-place awards for editorial car-
tooning by the Arkansas Press Association; editorial cartoonist for the
Arkansas Democrat-Gazette, 1988 to the present.

1994 OVERSEAS PRESS CLUB AWARD

MIKE LUCKOVICH
Editorial Cartoonist
Atlanta Constitution

Born January 28, 1960; editorial cartoonist for the *Greenville News,*
1984-85, the *New Orleans Times-Picayune,* 1985-89, and the *Atlanta
Constitution,* 1989 to the present; previous winner of the Overseas Press
Club Award, 1990; winner of the National Headliners Club Award, 1992,
and the Robert F. Kennedy Award, 1994; syndicated in 150 newspapers;
was the most frequently reprinted cartoonist in *Newsweek* for seven consecutive years.

MIKE THOMPSON
Editorial Cartoonist
Springfield State Journal-Register

Born in Mankato, Minnesota, 1964; graduate of the University of Wisconsin at Milwaukee; editorial cartoonist for the *St. Louis Sun,* 1989-90, and the Springfield, Illinois, *State Journal-Register,* 1990 to the present; syndicated by Copley News Service; winner of the Charles M. Schulz Award, 1988, and the John Locher Memorial Award, 1989.

BRUCE MACKINNON
Editorial Cartoonist
Halifax Herald

Native of Nova Scotia; studied fine arts at Mount Allison University
and the Nova Scotia College of Art and Design; editorial cartoonist for
the *Halifax Chronicle-Herald* and *Mail-Star,* 1985-86, and the *Halifax
Herald,* 1986 to the present; winner of the National Newspaper Award
of Canada in 1993 for the second consecutive year.

Best Editorial Cartoons of the Year

OSWALDO SAGASTEGUI
Courtesy Excelsior (Mex.)

The 1994 Election

As November approached, many pollsters acknowledged that the Republican party might win control of the Senate, but almost no one foresaw the full extent of the rout. The G.O.P. gained an astonishing fifty-one seats to gain control of the U.S. House of Representatives and picked up eight seats for a majority in the Senate. Across the nation not a single Republican congressional incumbent was defeated, while such Democratic icons as House Speaker Tom Foley, New York Gov. Mario Cuomo, and Texas Gov. Ann Richards were turned out of office.

The voters had clearly sent a message to Washington that they wanted less government, less taxes, and less welfare, and action on crime and the economy.

The Republican party seemed eager to deliver on its much-maligned Contract with America, promising to bring ten major issues to a vote in Congress. The new Speaker of the House, Rep. Newt Gingrich of Georgia, quickly began to draw the lines of battle.

Proposition 187, which denies illegal immigrants education and welfare benefits, passed in California, but was immediately challenged in court.

Many observers saw the 1994 election as a resounding vote of confidence for the policies of Ronald Reagan and a demand for a return to them. President Clinton had been leading a charge in the other direction.

STEVE BREEN
Courtesy Asbury Park Press (N.J.)

The Sandbag

15

BOB SHINGLETON
Courtesy Waterbury Republican-American

"LIES? YES! BUT THE GREAT COMMUNICATOR MADE ME DO IT!"

CHARLES BISSELL
Courtesy The Tennessean

WAYNE STROOT
Courtesy Hastings Tribune

CHARLES FAGAN
Courtesy Associated Features Syndicate

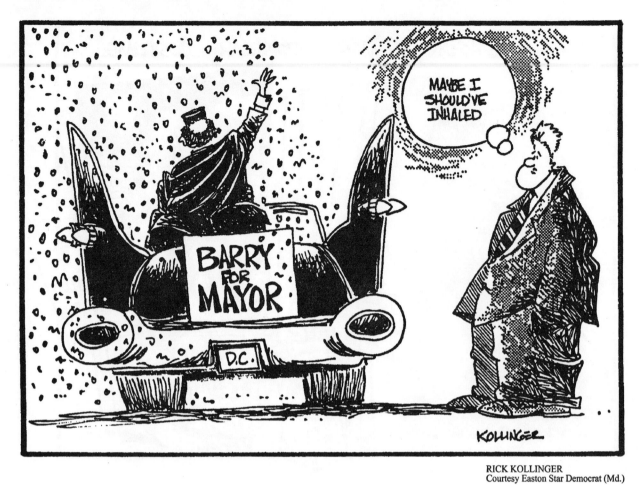

RICK KOLLINGER
Courtesy Easton Star Democrat (Md.)

DAVE COVERLY
Courtesy Bloomington Herald-Times

18

MARK BREWER
Courtesy The Hour (Conn.)

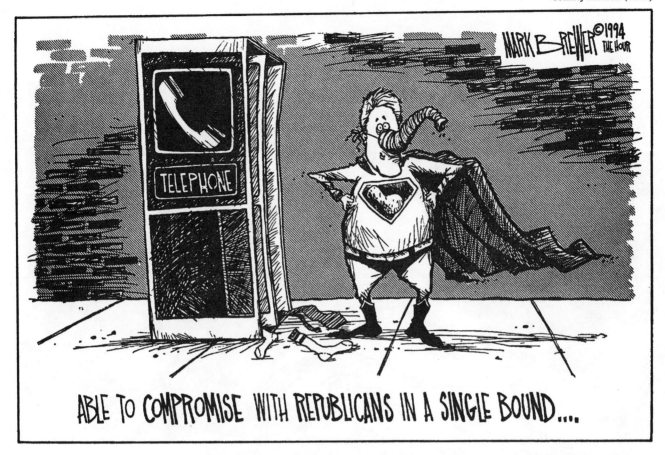

ABLE TO COMPROMISE WITH REPUBLICANS IN A SINGLE BOUND....

STEVE SACK
Courtesy Minneapolis Star-Tribune

BRIAN DUFFY
Courtesy Des Moines Register

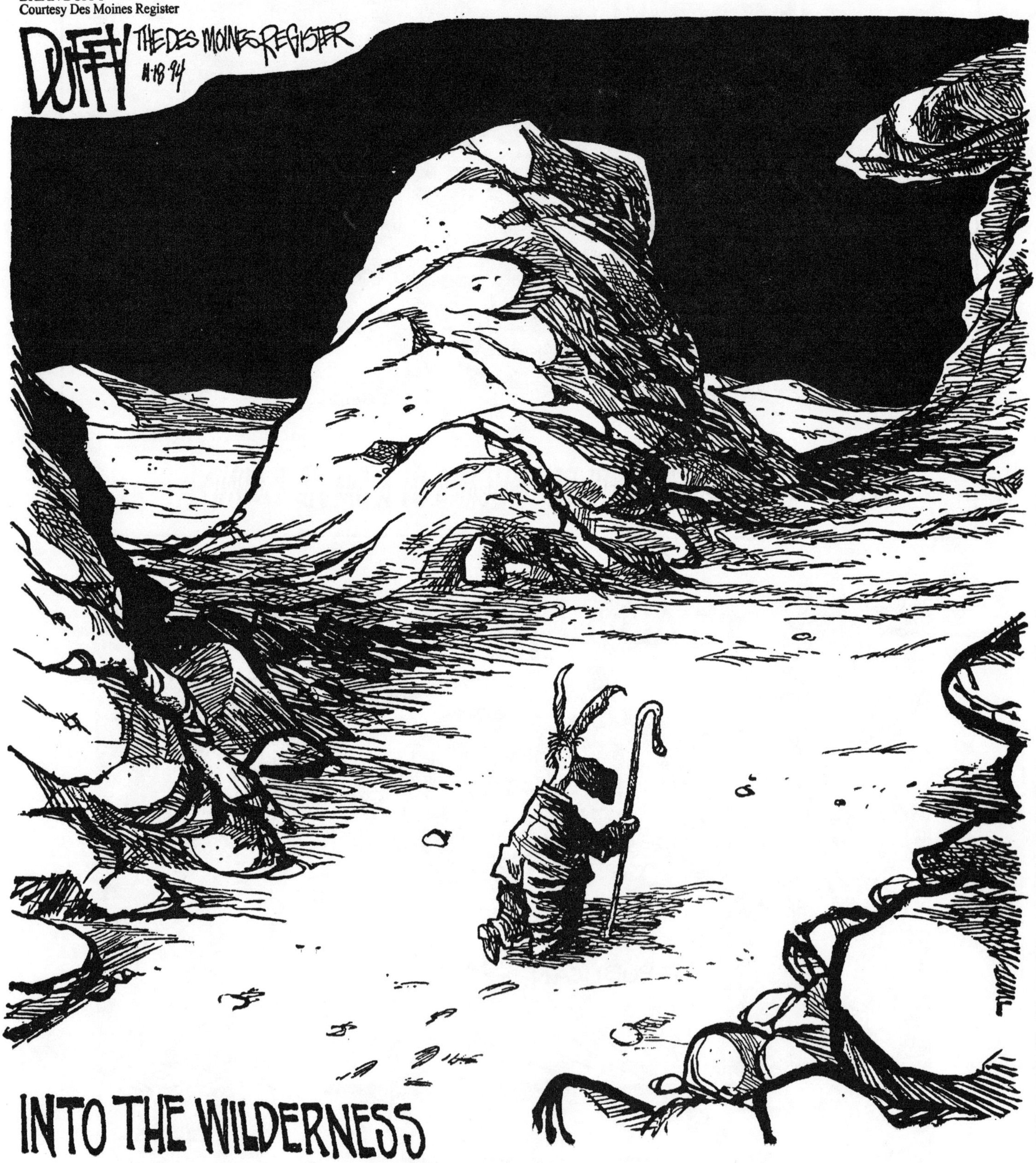
DUFFY THE DES MOINES REGISTER
11-18-94
INTO THE WILDERNESS

DICK WALLMEYER
Courtesy Long Beach Press-Telegram

JEFF MACNELLY
Courtesy Chicago Tribune and
Tribune Media Services

VOTERS OVERWHELMINGLY APPROVE PROPOSITION 187.

PAUL DUGINSKI
Courtesy Fresno Bee

ROMAN GENN
Courtesy Los Angeles Times

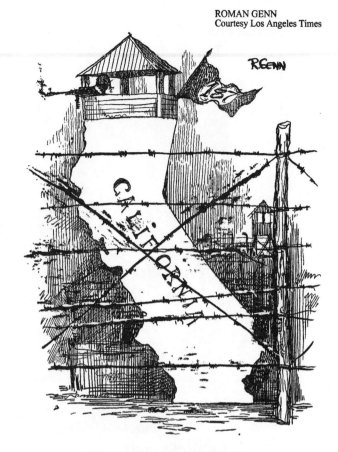

...THE LAND OF THE FREE...

THE GOOD NEWS IS ...
THAT TED KENNEDY HAS BEEN IN
THE US SENATE FOR 32 YEARS

THE BAD NEWS IS ...
THAT TED KENNEDY HAS BEEN IN
THE US SENATE FOR 32 YEARS

PAUL SZEP
Courtesy Boston Globe

SCOTT WILLIS
Courtesy San Jose Mercury

GARY VARVEL
Courtesy Indianapolis News

MARK CULLUM
Courtesy Birmingham News

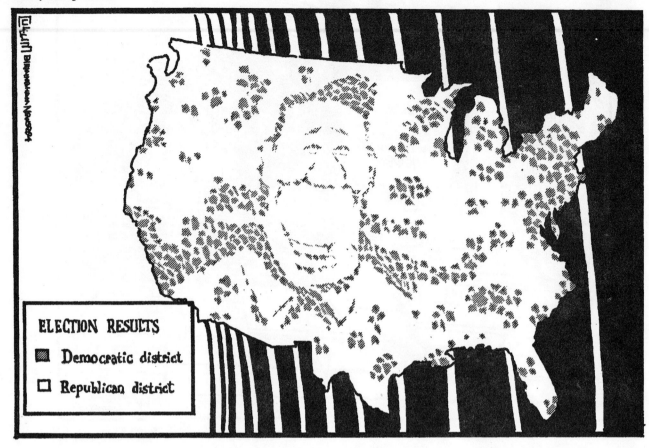

ELECTION RESULTS

▨ Democratic district

☐ Republican district

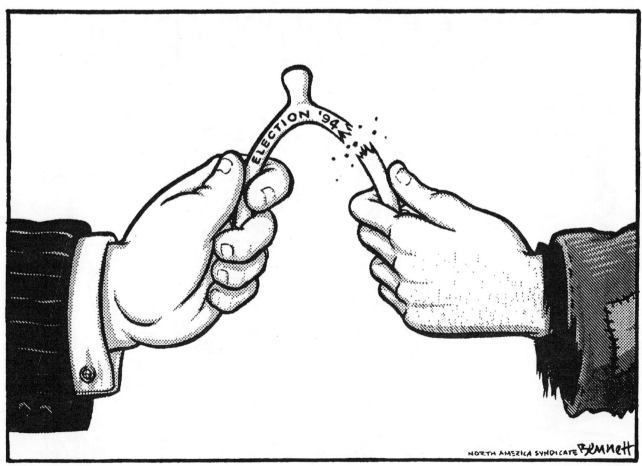

NORTH AMERICA SYNDICATE Bennett

CLAY BENNETT
Courtesy St. Petersburg Times

THAT'S <u>NEW</u> DEMOCRAT, YOU IDIOT!

FRANK CAMMUSO
Courtesy Syracuse Herald-Journal

TOM DARCY
Courtesy Newsday

"REMEMBER WHEN DEMOCRATIC INCUMBENTS USED TO ASK FOR VOTES BY WALKING THROUGH AND SHAKING HANDS?"

DANI AGUILA
Courtesy Filipino Reporter

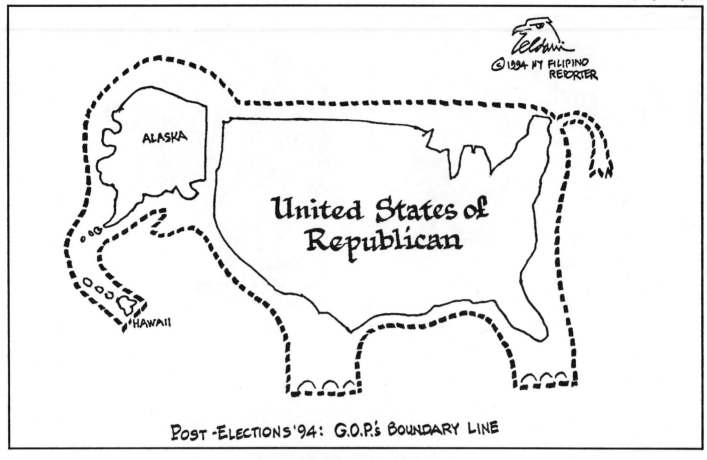

©1994 NY FILIPINO REPORTER

ALASKA

United States of Republican

HAWAII

POST-ELECTIONS '94: G.O.P.'s BOUNDARY LINE

MIDTERM ELECTIONS

REX BABIN TIMES UNION

REX BABIN
Courtesy Times Union (N.Y.)

RICHARD CROWSON
Courtesy Wichita Eagle

JEFF STAHLER
Courtesy Cincinnati Post

ANN CLEAVES
Courtesy La Prensa (San Diego)

DAVID GRANLUND
Courtesy Middlesex News

STEVE LINDSTROM
Courtesy Duluth News-Tribune

ROBERT ARIAIL
Courtesy The State (S.C.)

JEFF STAHLER
Courtesy Cincinnati Post

JACK JURDEN
Courtesy Wilmington News Journal

JOHN DEERING
Courtesy Arkansas Democrat-Gazette

"...WELL, I SAID I WAS THE PRESIDENT OF CHANGE..."

ED COLLEY
Courtesy Memorial Press Group

The Clinton Administration

Land dealings by the Clintons in a project called Whitewater back in Arkansas attracted the attention of special prosecutor Robert Fiske. Fiske issued a report in June that concluded that Clinton administration officials had committed no crimes and that the death of Clinton aide Vince Foster was a suicide. A new prosecutor, Kenneth Starr, was then appointed to probe the matter further, and Republicans declared they intended to get to the bottom of it. Clinton's approval rating in office sagged to near 40 percent toward the end of the year, and Democratic incumbents steered clear of him during the fall campaign.

A judge ruled that a suit filed against Clinton by Paula Jones for sexual advances would be delayed until he left office, but that Special Prosecutor Starr would have a right to question her before that time.

Eyebrows were raised when it was disclosed that Hillary Rodham Clinton had parlayed a few thousand dollars into a $100,000 profit by trading cattle futures. Mrs. Clinton insisted that her good fortune was based on studying the market and consulting with friends, but only the most die-hard Democrats accepted her explanation.

President Clinton named Judge Stephen Breyer the 108th justice of the U.S. Supreme Court. The administration insisted it had slashed spending, even though projections showed the deficit spiraling upward into the next century.

JACK OHMAN
Courtesy Portland Oregonian

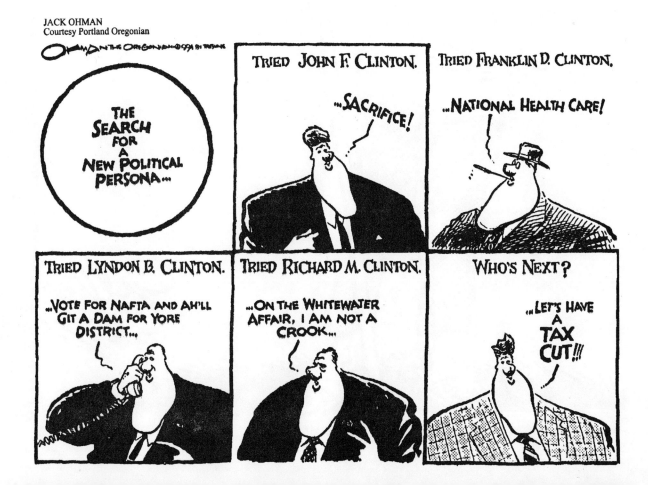

33

Clinton... 1968

HELL NO! I WON'T GO!

GILL FOX
Courtesy Connecticut Post

Clinton...1994

SOMALIA

BOSNIA

HAITI

GULF

MIKE THOMPSON
Courtesy State Journal-Register (Ill.)

THE SECRETARY OF STATE OF CONFUSION

PAUL SZEP
Courtesy Boston Globe

ROY PETERSON
Courtesy Vancouver Sun

MIKE PETERS
Courtesy Dayton Daily News

DALE STEPHANOS
Courtesy Haverhill Gazette (Mass.)

NICK ANDERSON
Courtesy Louisville Courier Journal

JOHN DEROSIER
Courtesy Mobile Press Register

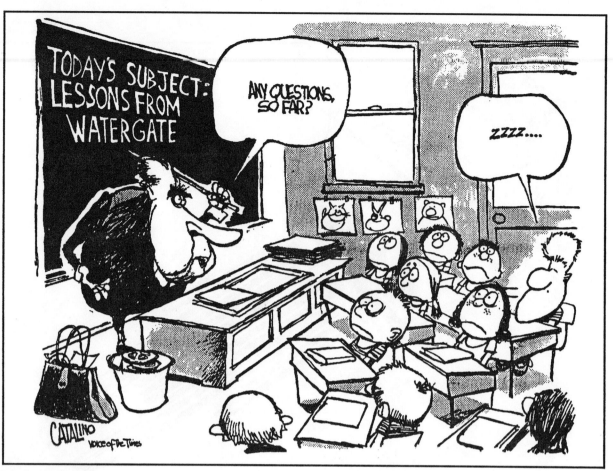

KEN CATALINO
Courtesy Anchorage Times

JERRY HOLBERT
Courtesy Boston Herald

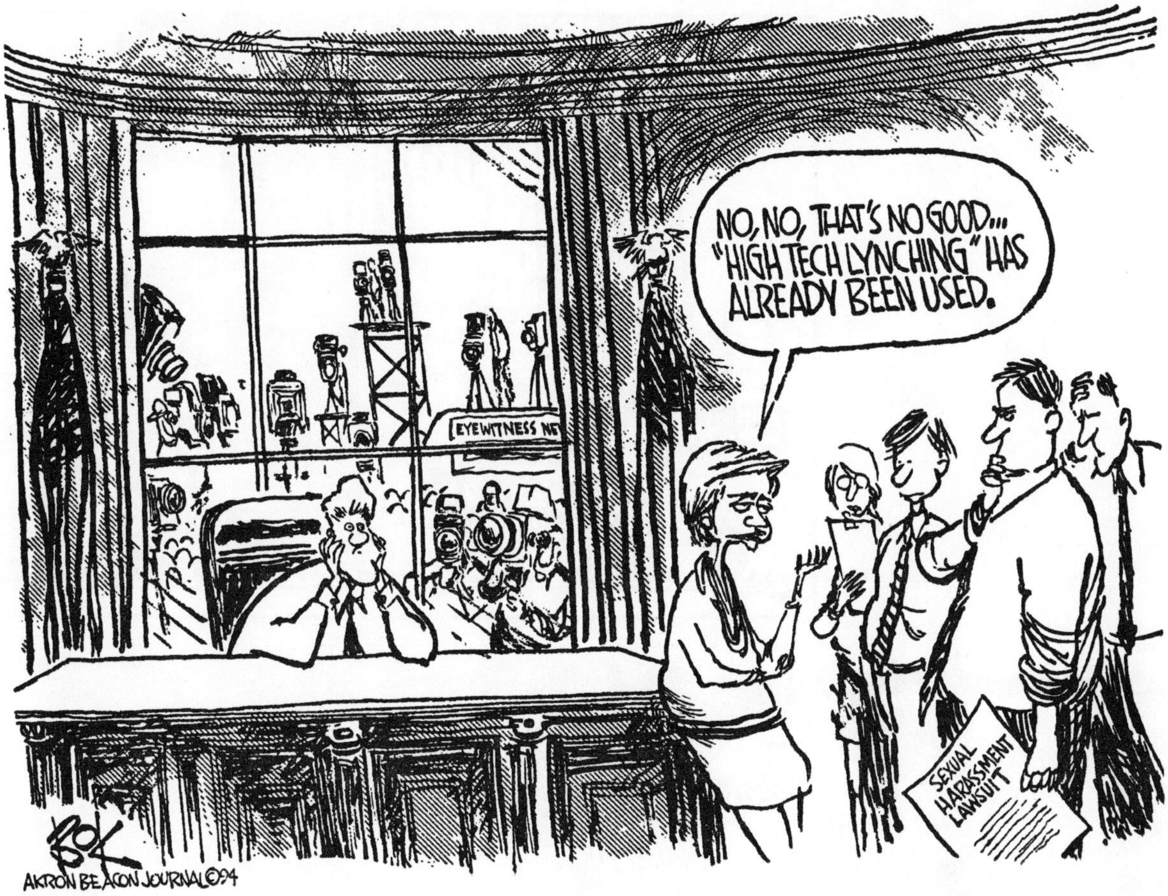
NO, NO, THAT'S NO GOOD... "HIGH TECH LYNCHING" HAS ALREADY BEEN USED.
EYEWITNESS NE
SEXUAL HARASSMENT LAWSUIT
BOK
AKRON BEACON JOURNAL ©94

CHIP BOK
Courtesy Akron Beacon Journal

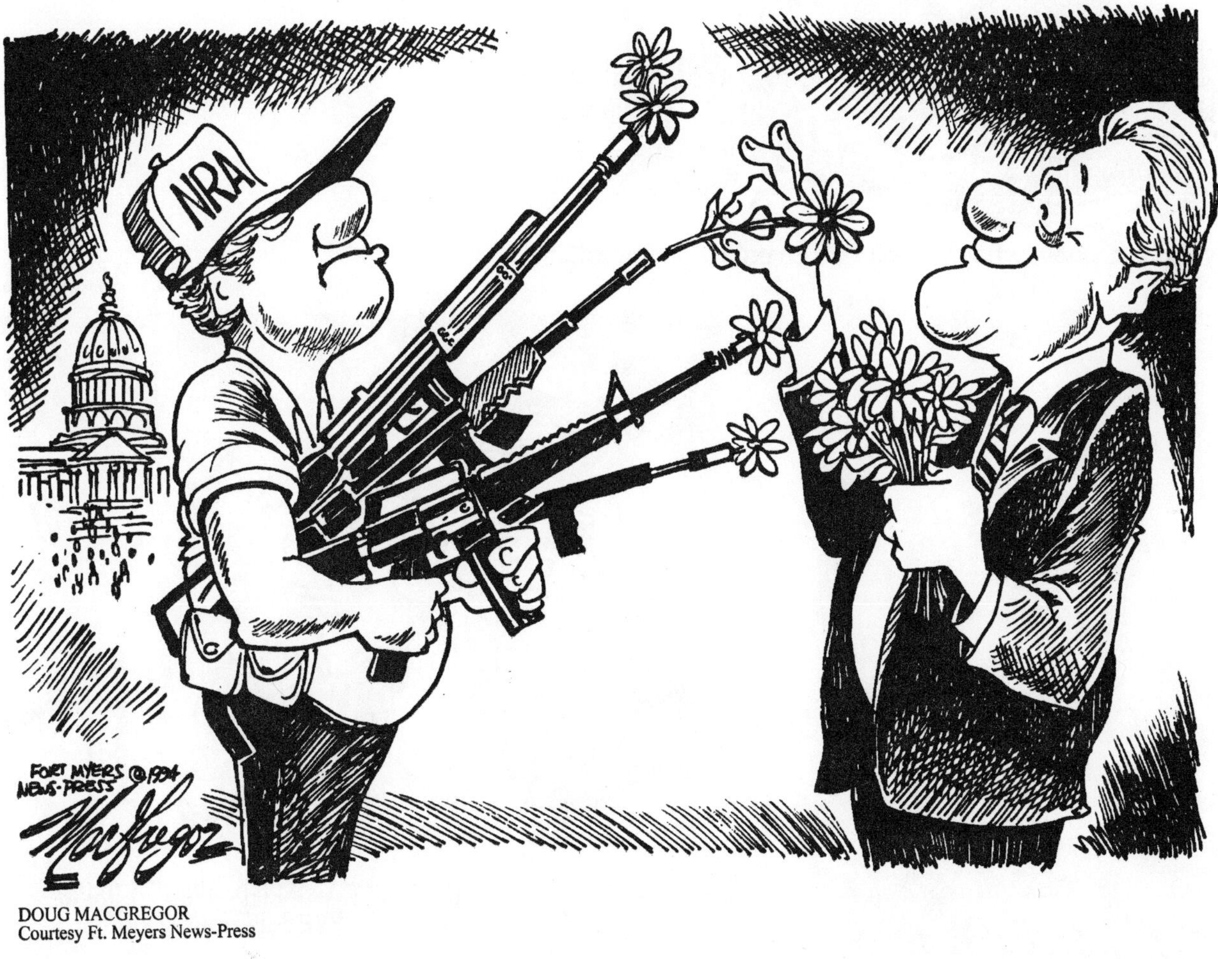
NRA
FORT MYERS ©1994 NEWS-PRESS
MacGregor

DOUG MACGREGOR
Courtesy Ft. Meyers News-Press

"Hey, honey... guess what?...I still fit into my old uniform!..."

THE ONLY PERSON NOT WORRIED ABOUT LOSING
HIS BAGGAGE AT DENVER INTERNATIONAL...

ROBERT ARIAIL
Courtesy The State (S.C.)

CHUCK ASAY
Courtesy Colorado Springs Gazette Telegraph

ED GAMBLE
Courtesy Florida Times-Union

GARY VARVEL
Courtesy Indianapolis News

STUART CARLSON
Courtesy Milwaukee Sentinel

RANDY BISH
Courtesy Tribune-Review (Pa.)

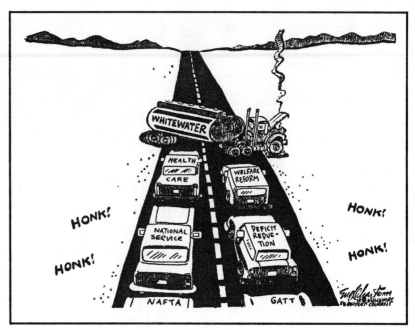

BOB ENGLEHART
Courtesy Hartford Courant

BILL GARNER
Courtesy Washington Times

BONNIE AND CLOD

BOB LANG
Courtesy News-Sentinel (Ind.)

LAMBERT DER
Courtesy Houston Post

JOHN SPENCER
Courtesy Philadelphia Business Journal

GARY BROOKINS
Courtesy Richmond Times-Dispatch

JOE HELLER
Courtesy Green Bay Press-Gazette

ROGER SCHILLERSTROM
Courtesy Crain Communications

BRUCE BEATTIE
Courtesy Daytona Beach News-Journal

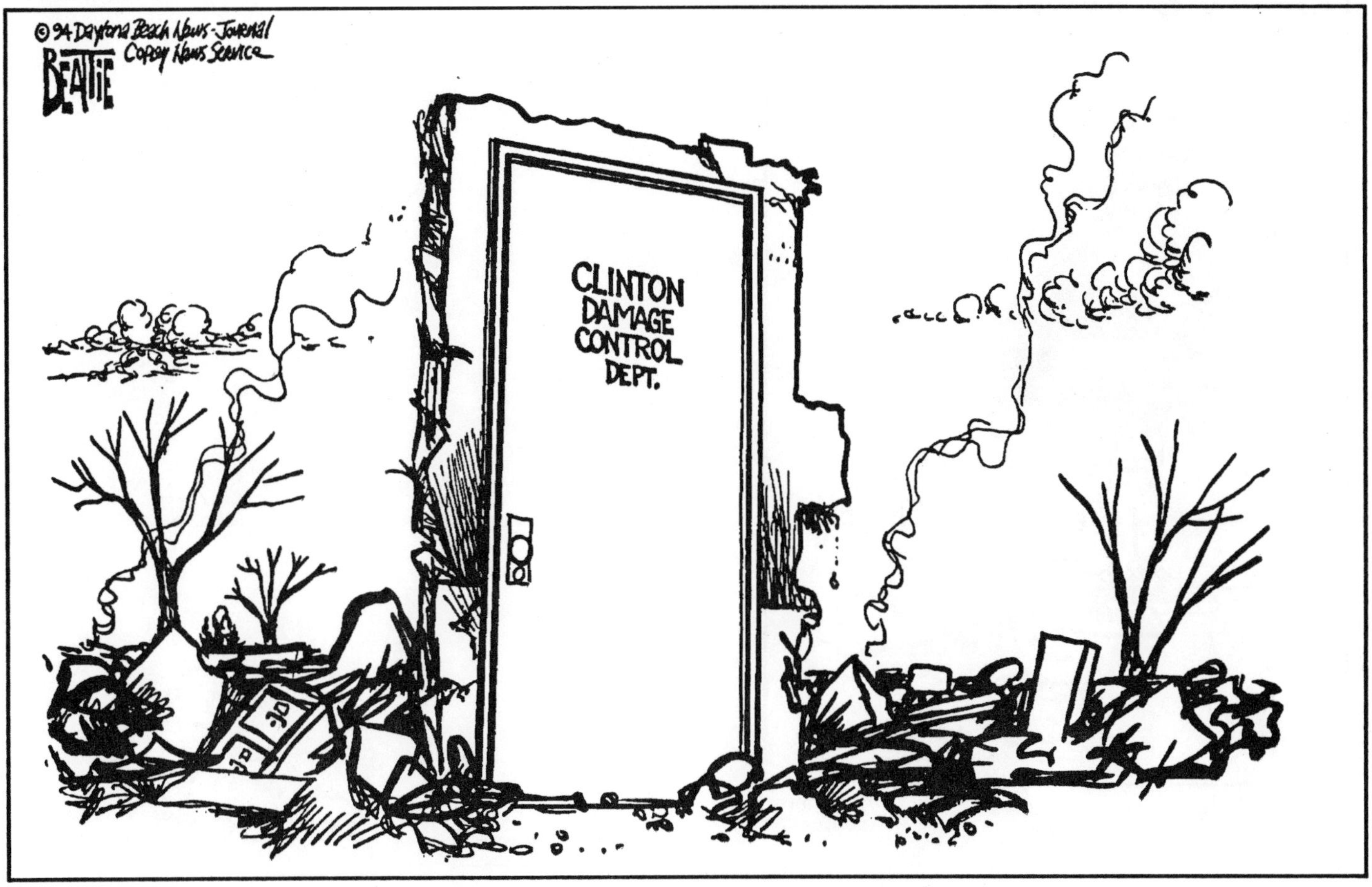
© 94 Daytona Beach News-Journal Copley News Service
BEATTIE
CLINTON DAMAGE CONTROL DEPT.

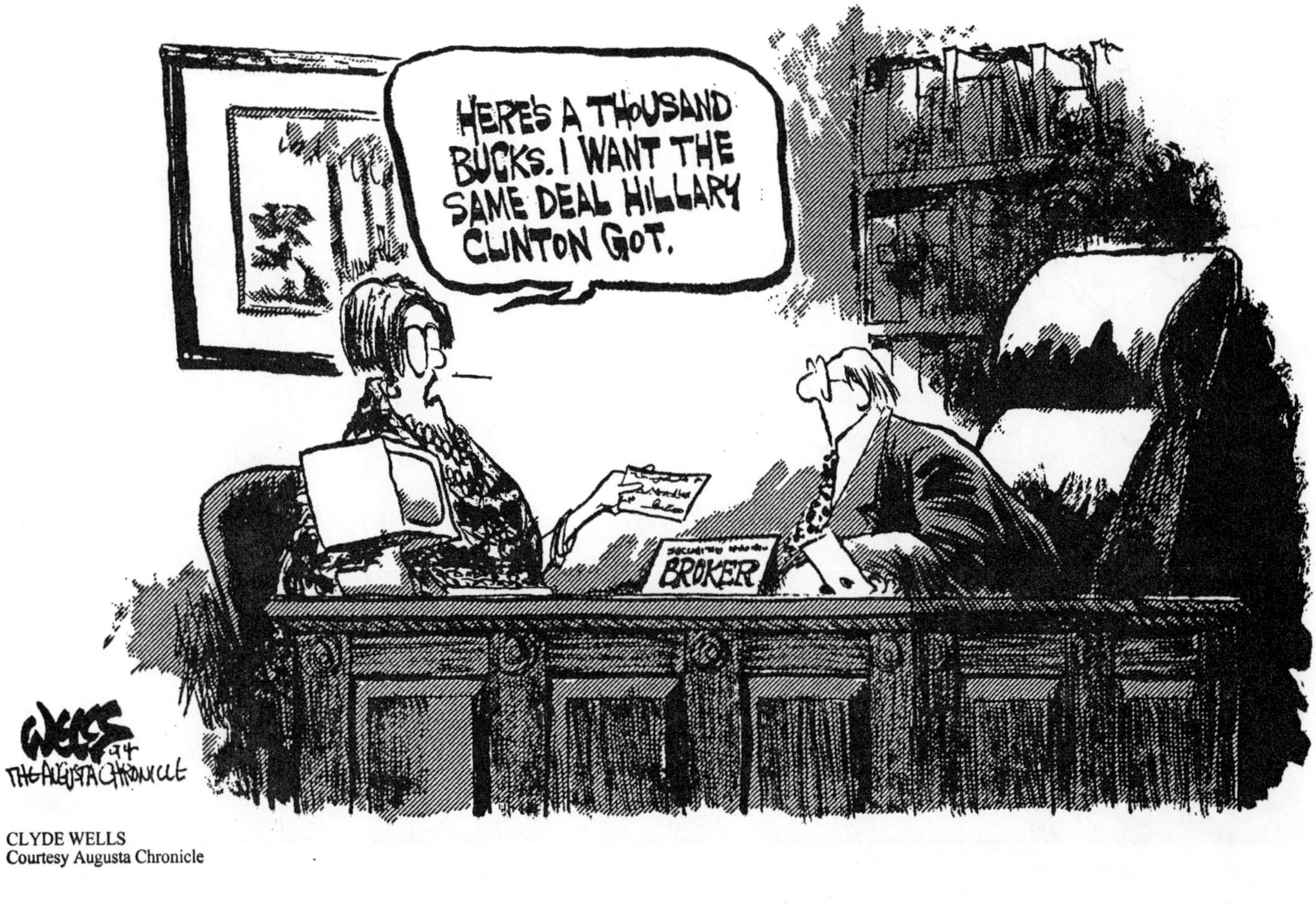
HERE'S A THOUSAND BUCKS. I WANT THE SAME DEAL HILLARY CLINTON GOT.
BROKER
WELLS '94 THE AUGUSTA CHRONICLE

CLYDE WELLS
Courtesy Augusta Chronicle

Berry's World

JIM BERRY
Courtesy NEA

EDD ULUSCHAK
Courtesy The Sounder

JERRY HUGHES
Courtesy Enterprise-Ledger (Ala.)

ED GAMBLE
Courtesy Florida Times-Union

WALLS OF JERICHO

PAUL CONRAD
Courtesy Los Angeles Times

Foreign Affairs

On April 26, 1994, apartheid ended in South Africa as blacks voted in free elections for the first time. Nelson Mandela, leader of the African National Congress and for many years a prisoner of the government, was elected prime minister.

The flood of refugees from Haiti and Cuba to the United States continued in 1994. Near the end of the summer, the Clinton administration threatened to invade Haiti and remove army commander Lt. Gen. Raoul Cedras by force. Last-minute talks between Haitian leaders and a U.S. delegation led by former president Jimmy Carter, however, produced a solution of sorts. Ousted Haitian president Jean-Bertrand Aristide was allowed to resume office, Cedras was permitted to remain in the country, and 20,000 U.S. troops entered the country as a peace-keeping force.

Cubans kept trying to reach U.S. shores until an agreement was reached that persuaded most to remain at home. The horrible killing continued in Rwanda, with more than a million believed dead and millions more becoming refugees. The U.S. pulled troops out of Somalia early in the year, leaving behind a rapidly deteriorating situation.

At year's end, the U.S. and Europe were still at odds over how to end the killing in Bosnia. Britain's Prince Charles shocked his countrymen when he admitted in a new book that he had been unfaithful to Princess Diana.

JACK HIGGINS
Courtesy Chicago Sun-Times

53

BILL GARNER
Courtesy Washington Times

ORIENT EXPRESSIONS

CLYDE WELLS
Courtesy Augusta Chronicle

DICK LOCHER
Courtesy Chicago Tribune

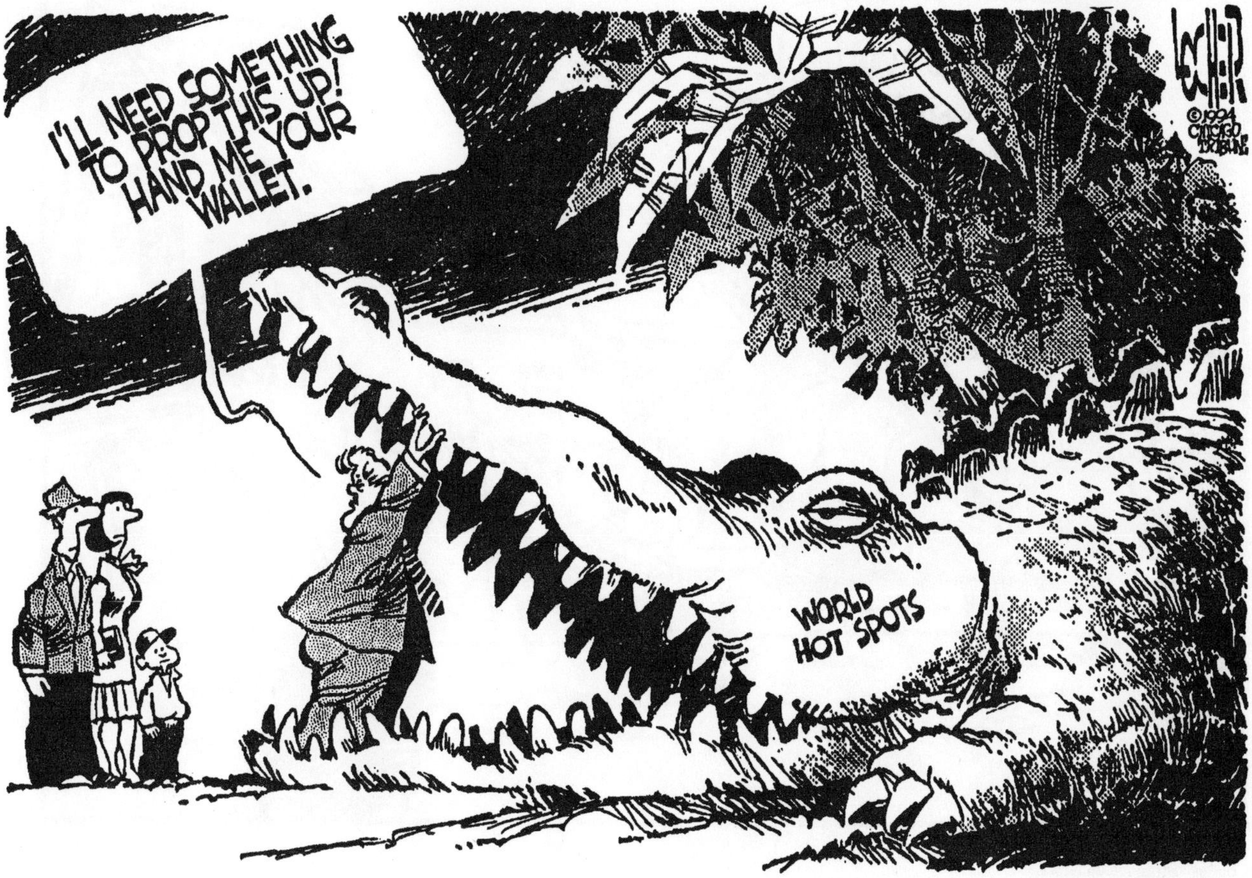
I'LL NEED SOMETHING TO PROP THIS UP! HAND ME YOUR WALLET.
WORLD HOT SPOTS
©1994 CHICAGO TRIBUNE

NICK ANDERSON
Courtesy Louisville Courier Journal

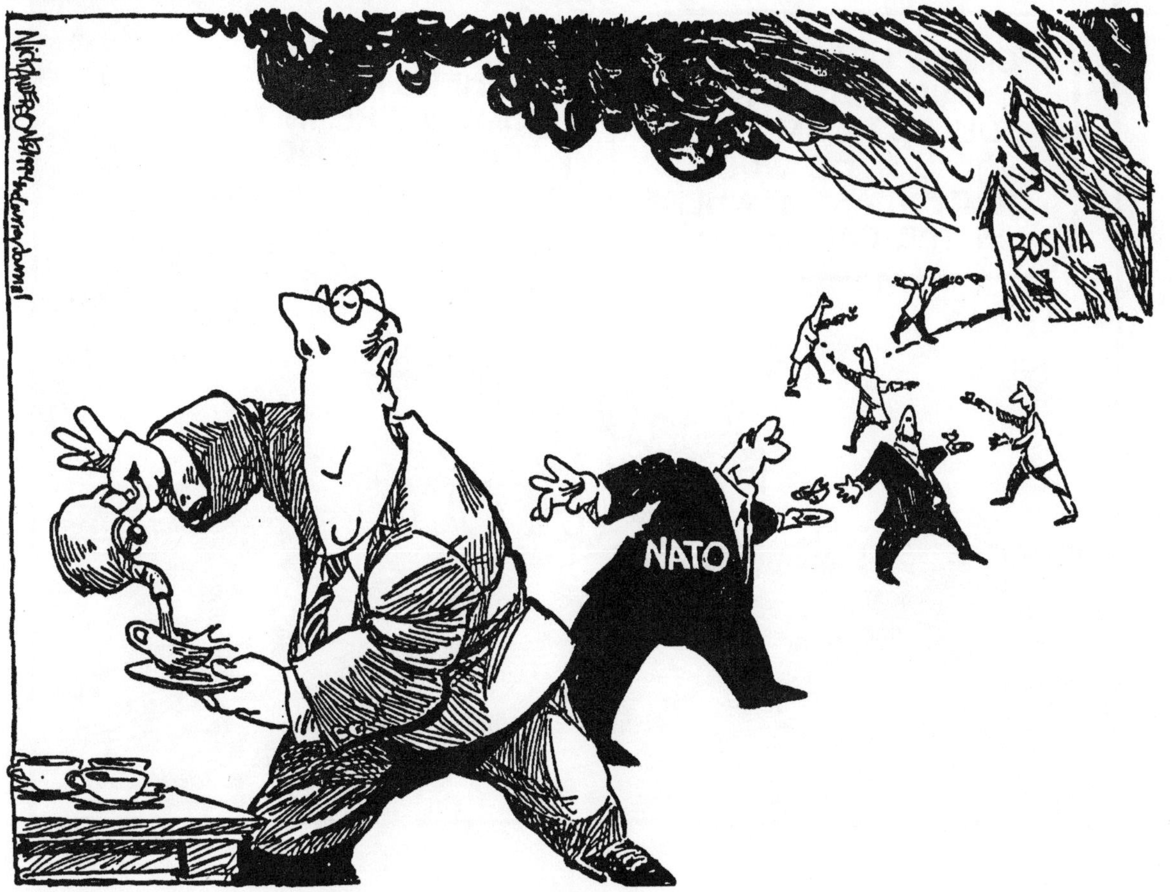
BOSNIA
NATO

MARK CULLUM
Courtesy Birmingham News

STEVE SCALLION
Courtesy Arkansas Democrat-Gazette

KEVIN SIERS
Courtesy Charlotte Observer

DECLINE AND FALL OF THE BRITISH MONARCHY

CHAN LOWE
Courtesy The News/Sun-Sentinel (Fla.)

Berry's World

"Things are really looking up here these days — if you're in the MAFIA."

JIM BERRY
Courtesy NEA

FRED SEBASTIAN
Courtesy Ottawa Citizen

GUY BADEAUX
Courtesy Le Droit (Ottawa)

OSWALDO SAGASTEGUI
Courtesy Excelsior (Mex.)

DENNY PRITCHARD
Courtesy Ottawa Citizen

MIKE PETERS
Courtesy Dayton Daily News

JOHN DEROSIER
Courtesy Mobile Press Register

DAVID GRANLUND
Courtesy Middlesex News

DAVID GRANLUND
Courtesy Middlesex News

JERRY HOLBERT
Courtesy Boston Herald

DENNIS DRAUGHON
Courtesy Scranton Times

JOHN TREVER
Courtesy Albuquerque Journal

BRIAN DUFFY
Courtesy Des Moines Register

FRED CURATOLO
Courtesy Edmonton Sun

GEORGE DANBY
Courtesy Bangor Daily News

JOE HELLER
Courtesy Green Bay Press-Gazette

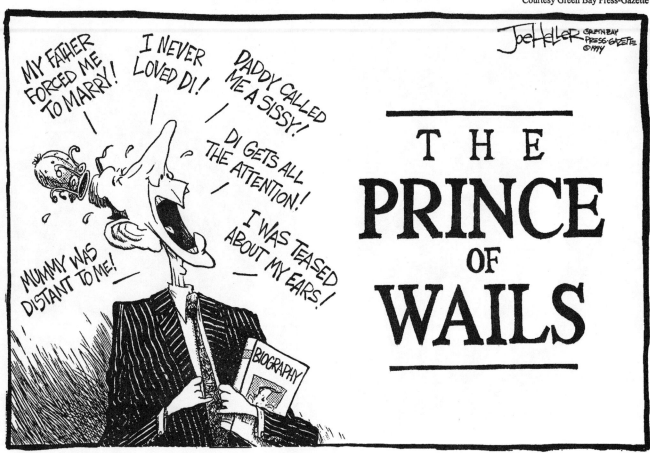

THE
PRINCE
OF
WAILS

ROY PETERSON
Courtesy Vancouver Sun

RUSSIA'S COMMODITY EXCHANGE!

BE ALL THAT YOU CAN BE

THE CLINTSTONES

BRINGING HUMAN RIGHTS
BACK TO THE STONE AGE

"WHERE ARE YOU, MR. SCHINDLER?"

JOHN BRANCH
Courtesy San Antonio Express-News

ROBERT ARIAIL
Courtesy The State (S.C.)

JOE LONG
Courtesy Little Falls Evening Times (N.Y.)

IN THE FIFTH CENTURY, ST. PATRICK DROVE THE SNAKES OUT OF IRELAND...

...SOME SNAKES STILL REMAIN.

LAMBERT DER
Courtesy Houston Post

MICHAEL FAY, THE WORLD IS HOLDING ITS BREATH: DOES YOUR TUSH HURT?!

THE CANE MUTINY

DANI AGUILA
Courtesy Filipino Reporter

PRISONER, 1963-1990

PRESIDENT, 1994-

PAUL SZEP
Courtesy Boston Globe

THE HOLY HATERS

JAMES MERCADO
Courtesy Honolulu Star-Bulletin

GLEN FODEN
Courtesy Patuxent Pub. Co.

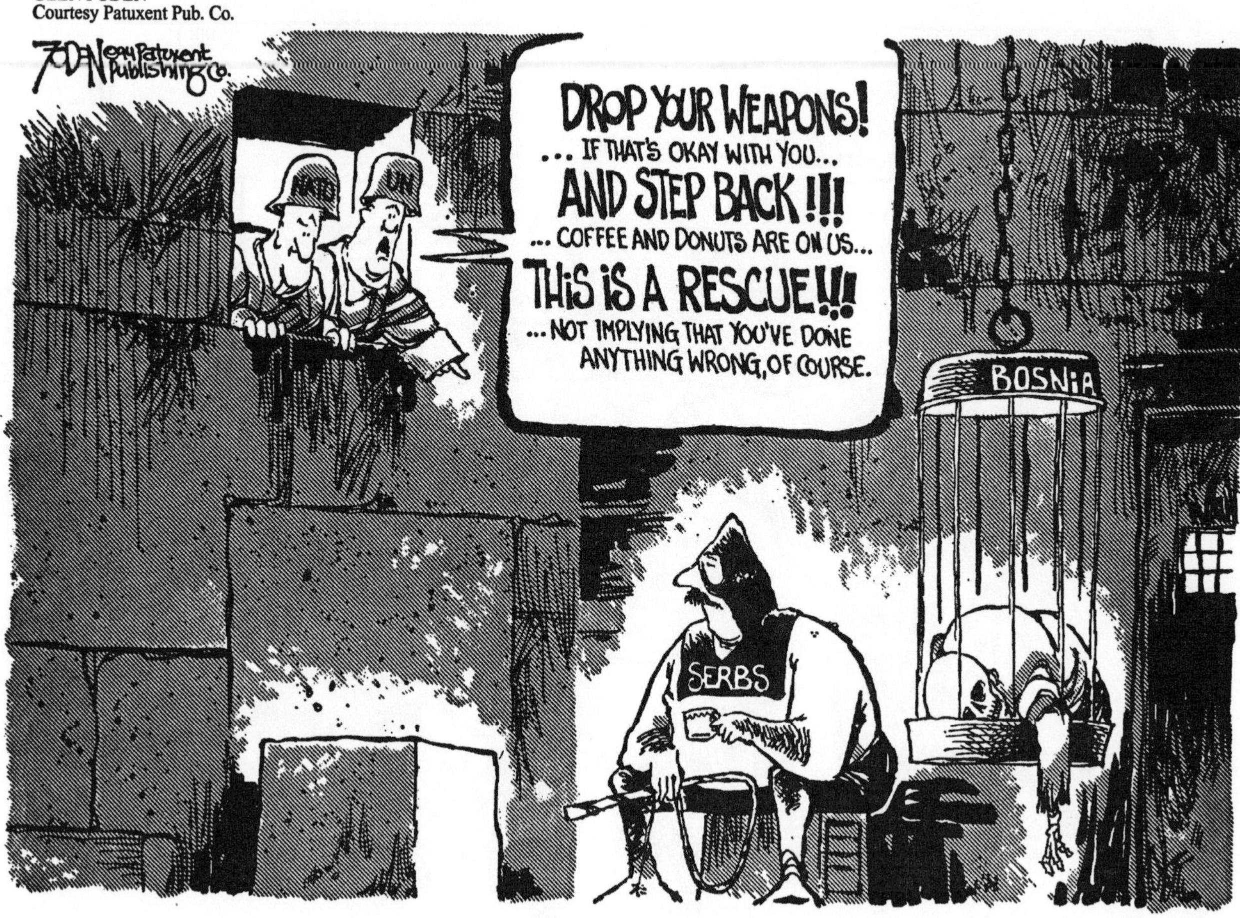
FODEN ©Patuxent Publishing Co.
DROP YOUR WEAPONS!
... IF THAT'S OKAY WITH YOU...
AND STEP BACK!!!
... COFFEE AND DONUTS ARE ON US...
THIS IS A RESCUE!!!
... NOT IMPLYING THAT YOU'VE DONE ANYTHING WRONG, OF COURSE.
NATO
UN
BOSNIA
SERBS

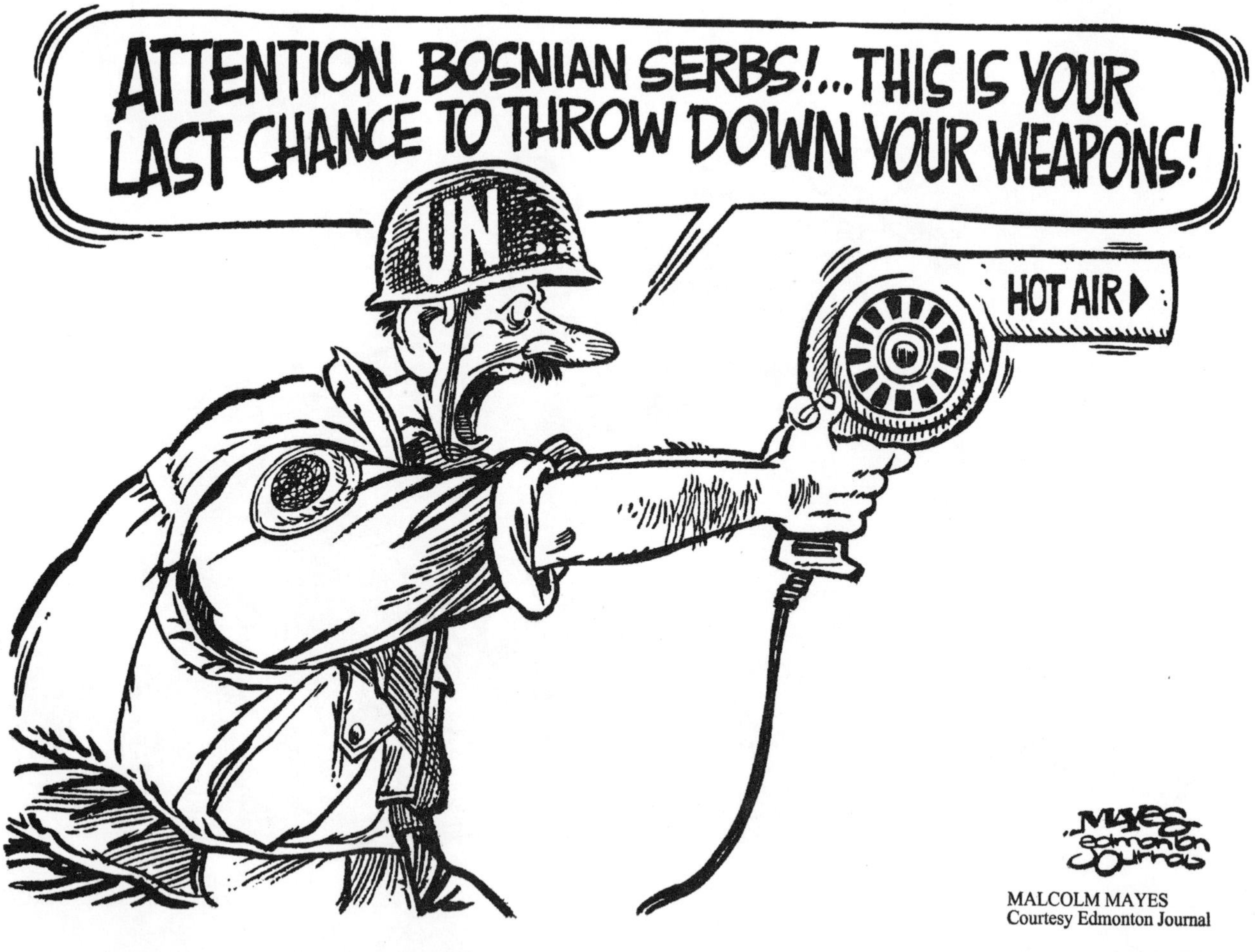
ATTENTION, BOSNIAN SERBS!...THIS IS YOUR LAST CHANCE TO THROW DOWN YOUR WEAPONS!
UN
HOT AIR
MAYES Edmonton Journal

MALCOLM MAYES
Courtesy Edmonton Journal

PAUL CONRAD
Courtesy Los Angeles Times

A FISH CALLED RWANDA

WICKS
© THE SIGNAL 1994

RANDY WICKS
Courtesy Valencia Signal (Calif.)

BRUCE MACKINNON
Courtesy Halifax Chronicle-Herald

MIKE KEEFE
Courtesy Denver Post

JERRY BARNETT
Courtesy Indianapolis News

STEVE NEASE
Courtesy Ottawa Citizen

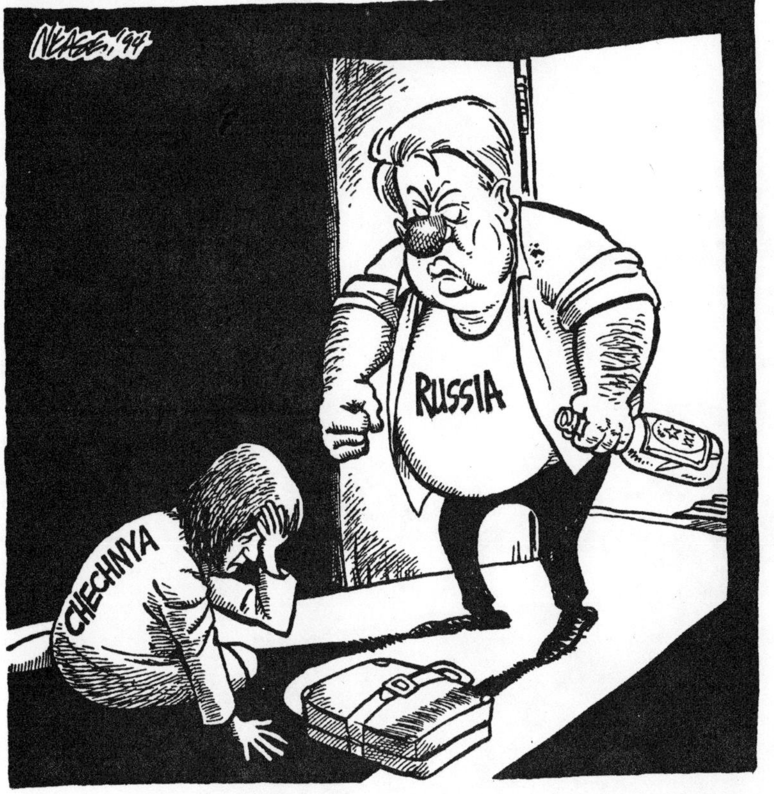
NEASE '97
RUSSIA
CHECHNYA

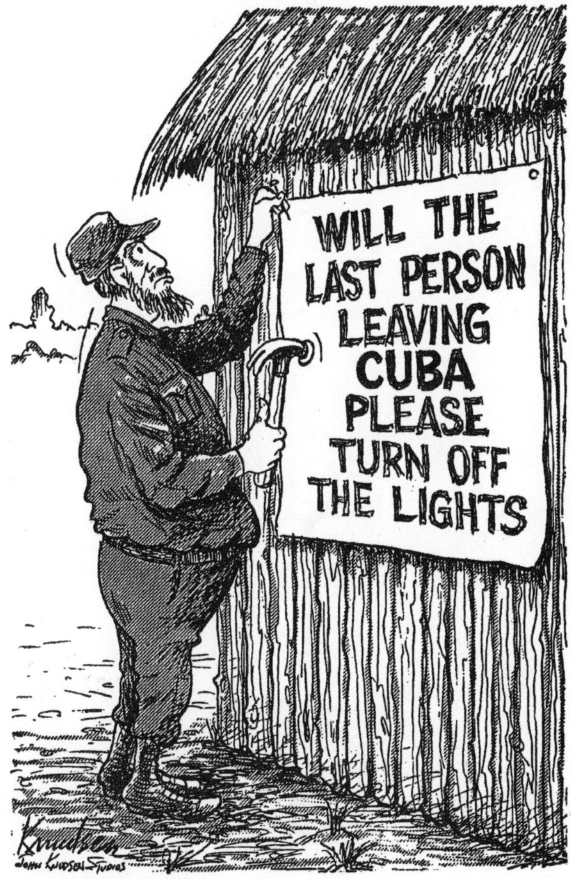
WILL THE
LAST PERSON
LEAVING
CUBA
PLEASE
TURN OFF
THE LIGHTS
Knudsen
John Knudsen Studios

JOHN KNUDSEN
Courtesy The Tidings (Calif.)

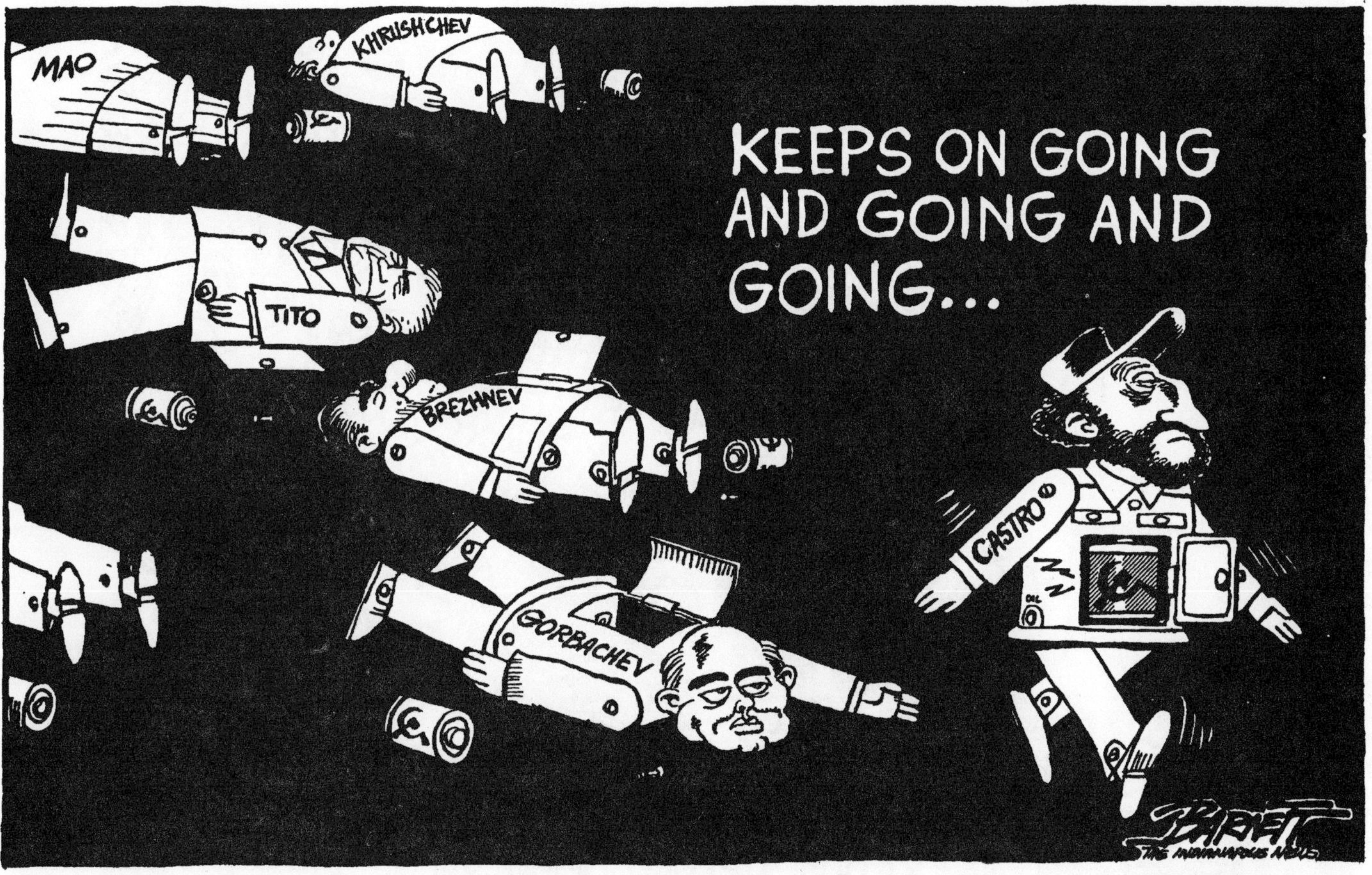
MAO
KHRUSHCHEV
KEEPS ON GOING
AND GOING AND
GOING...
TITO
BREZHNEV
CASTRO
GORBACHEV
BARNETT
THE INDIANAPOLIS NEWS

JERRY BARNETT
Courtesy Indianapolis News

DRAPER HILL
Courtesy Detroit News

JOHN TREVER
Courtesy Albuquerque Journal

Berry's World

KING OF THE MOUNTAIN

JIM BERRY
Courtesy NEA

FRED CURATOLO
Courtesy Edmonton Sun

"YOU'RE FREE!... MIGHTY BIG OF ME, ISN'T IT?!"

BOB GORRELL
Courtesy Richmond Times-Dispatch/
Copley News Service

MADE IN AMERICA

PAUL CONRAD
Courtesy Los Angeles Times

GUNS DON'T KILL PEOPLE

PEOPLE WITH EASY ACCESS TO CHEAP, LOOSELY REGULATED, WILDLY POWERFUL GUNS DESIGNED SOLELY TO KILL PEOPLE KILL PEOPLE

JOHN KOVALIC
Courtesy Wisconsin State Journal

Crime

CIA agent Aldrich Ames was arrested for selling government secrets to the Soviet Union, prompting charges that officials at the supersecret agency had been asleep at the job. Ames' alleged betrayal was said to have destroyed the CIA's network of spies in the Soviet Union and to have caused the execution of ten agents.

In a celebrated case, Lorena Bobbitt was found not guilty of having cut off her husband's private parts, even though she admitted that she had done it. In Singapore, an American youngster was sentenced to an official caning for having been involved in wanton mischief. Some Americans were outraged by the sentence, but many crime-ridden citizens suggested that caning offenders might serve justice well in the U.S.

President Clinton's watered-down crime bill was finally passed by Congress, although the measure contained large expenditures for such social programs as midnight basketball leagues. One popular portion of the bill was the "Three Strikes and You're Out" provision on criminal convictions.

Four persons, including two doctors, were killed at abortion clinics as anti-abortion protests erupted into violence. A report showed that arrests for juvenile violent crimes increased 82 percent from 1982 to 1992 as more and more youngsters were carrying guns—and using them.

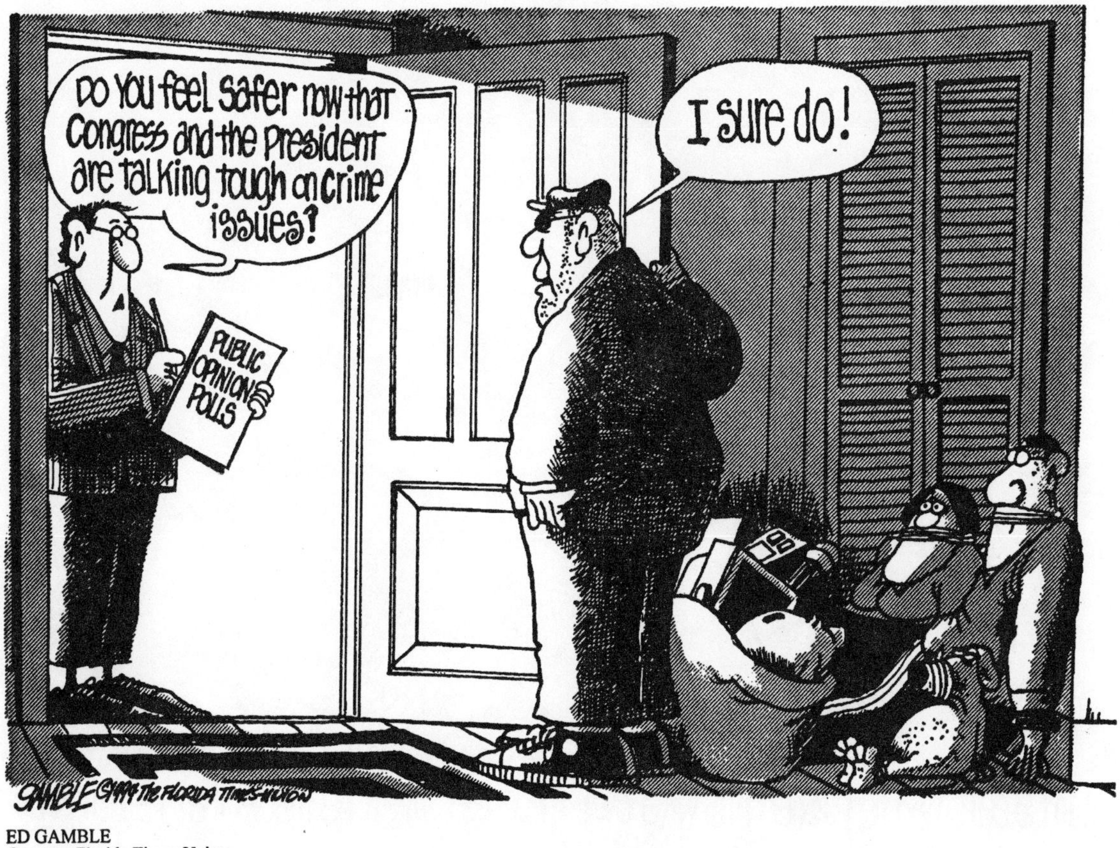
DO YOU FEEL SAFER NOW THAT CONGRESS AND THE PRESIDENT ARE TALKING TOUGH ON CRIME ISSUES?
I SURE DO!
PUBLIC OPINION POLLS

ED GAMBLE
Courtesy Florida Times-Union

MIKE PETERS
Courtesy Dayton Daily News

LET THE JURY NOTE THAT MRS. BOBBITT HAS IDENTIFIED HER **KNIFE** AS EXHIBIT Ⓐ.....

ED GAMBLE
Courtesy Florida Times-Union

He couldn't sleep... had he pushed his wife "over the edge" when he made that remark about her casserole?

MIKE LUCKOVICH
Courtesy Atlanta Constitution

ED FISCHER
Courtesy Rochester Post-Bulletin

DICK WRIGHT
Courtesy Providence Journal-Bulletin

JACK OHMAN
Courtesy Portland Oregonian

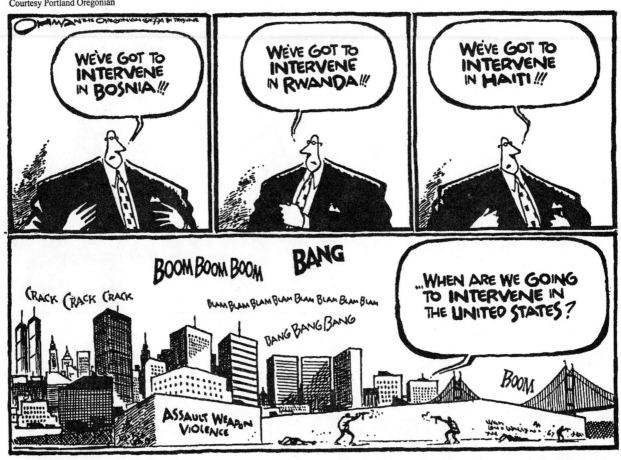

CHUCK ASAY
Courtesy Colorado Springs Gazette Telegraph

REX BABIN
Courtesy Times Union (N.Y.)

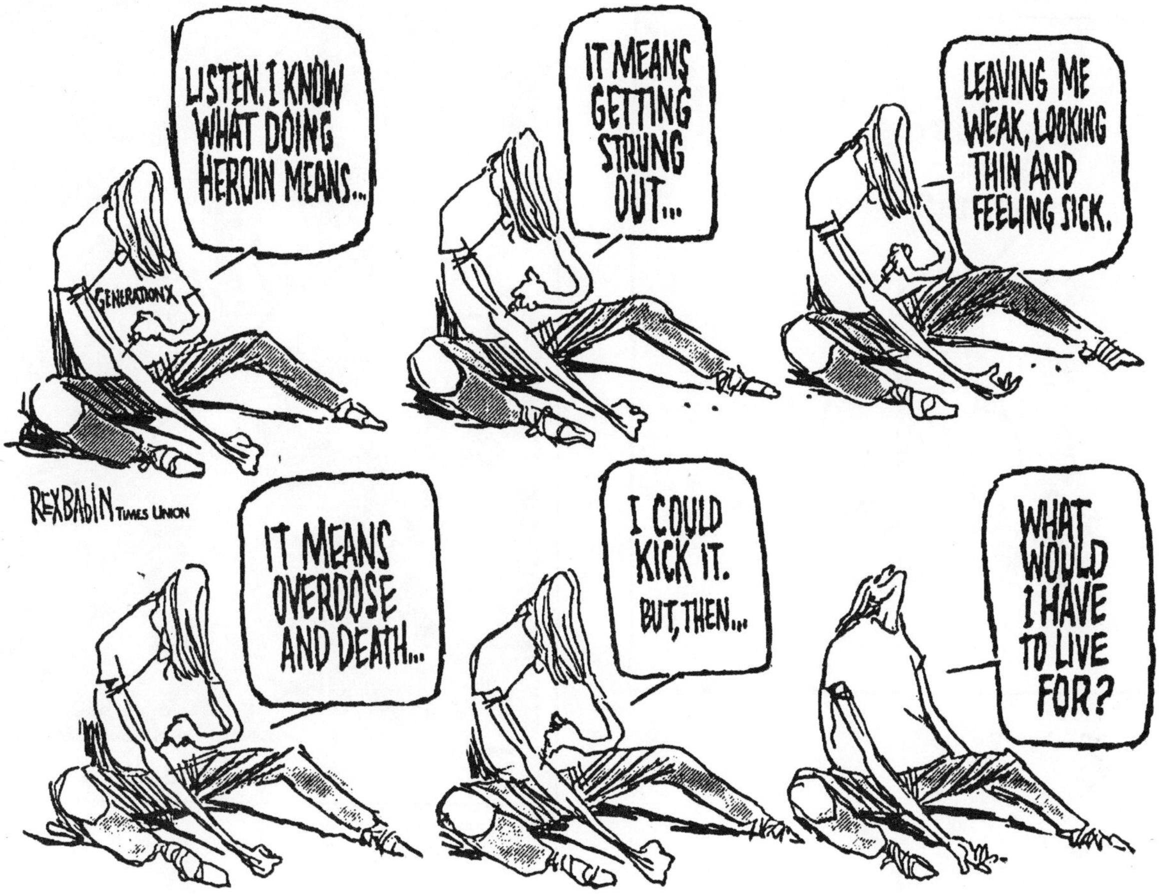
LISTEN. I KNOW WHAT DOING HEROIN MEANS...
GENERATION X
IT MEANS GETTING STRUNG OUT...
LEAVING ME WEAK, LOOKING THIN AND FEELING SICK.
REX BABIN TIMES UNION
IT MEANS OVERDOSE AND DEATH...
I COULD KICK IT. BUT, THEN...
WHAT WOULD I HAVE TO LIVE FOR?

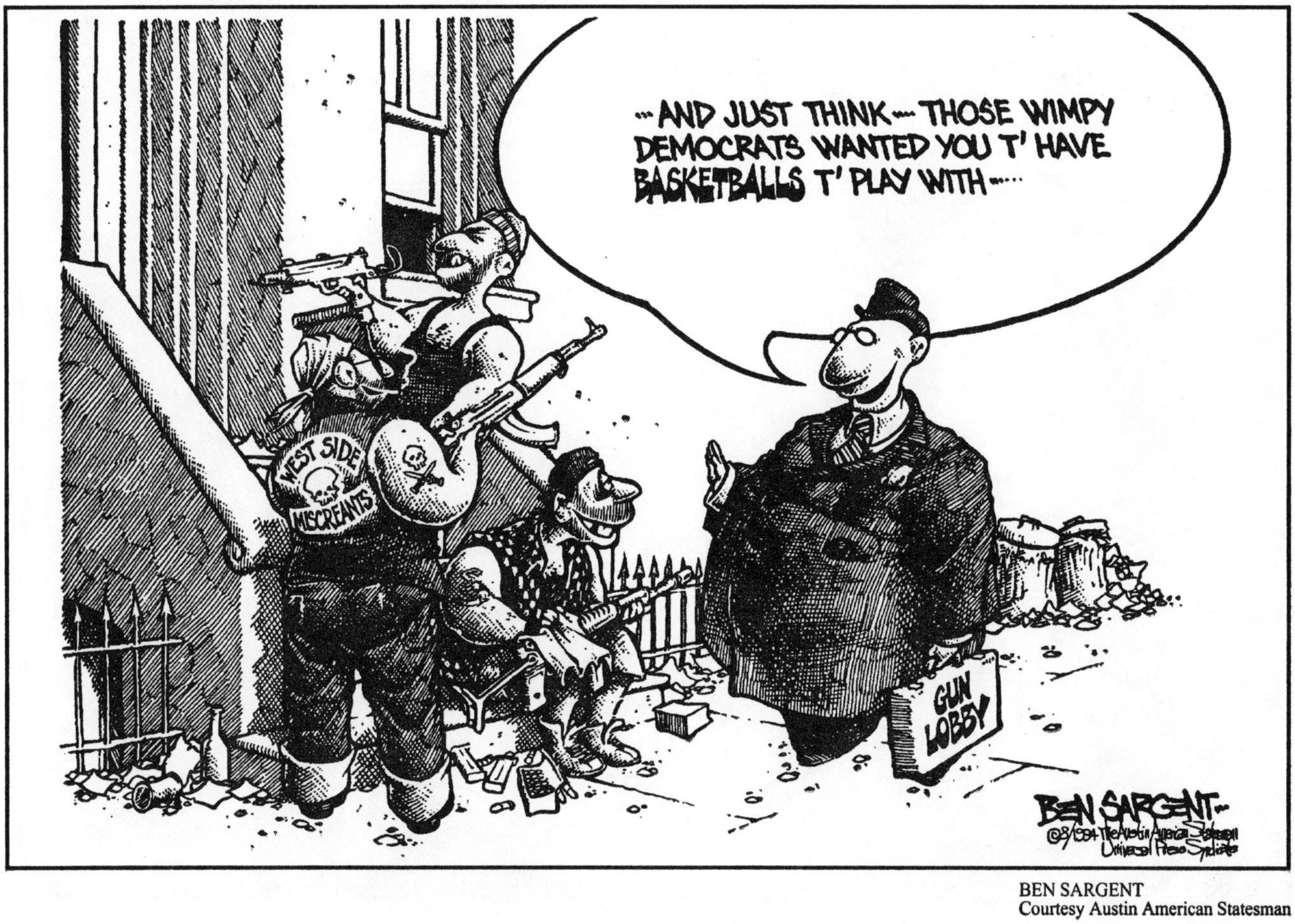
...AND JUST THINK... THOSE WIMPY DEMOCRATS WANTED YOU T' HAVE BASKETBALLS T' PLAY WITH.....
WEST SIDE MISCREANTS
GUN LOBBY
BEN SARGENT

BEN SARGENT
Courtesy Austin American Statesman

STEPHEN TEMPLETON
Courtesy National Forum/Associated Features

DENNIS RENAULT
Courtesy Sacramento Bee

Speaking of assisted suicide . . .

CLAY BENNETT
Courtesy St. Petersburg Times

JACK OHMAN
Courtesy Portland Oregonian

MIKE SMITH
Courtesy Las Vegas Sun

FOR SEVERAL YEARS, NO ONE AT THE CIA NOTICED THAT EMPLOYEE ALDRICH AMES WAS A MOLE.

Which deterrent is more effective?

JACK HIGGINS
Courtesy Chicago Sun-Times

WHAT DO YOU...

WANT TO BE...

WHEN YOU GRO—

BANG

TWELVE BLIND MICE, TWELVE BLIND MICE...

BOBBITT JURY

..SEE WHAT THEY'VE DONE? SEE WHAT THEY'VE DONE?..

LORENA BOBBITT VERDICT

...THEY FAILED TO CONVICT THE BOBBITT WIFE, WHO CUT OFF JOHN'S ___ WITH A KITCHEN KNIFE...

HAVE MEN EVER HAD SUCH A FRIGHT IN THEIR LIFE, FROM TWELVE BLIND MICE?

YIKES!

JURY: NO SENTENCE FOR SPOUSE SPLICER

MIKE THOMPSON
Courtesy State Journal-Register (Ill.)

"THEY'VE AMENDED THE CRIME BILL: TWO YEARS AND YOU'RE OUT!"

ERIC SMITH
Courtesy Capital Gazette Newspapers

CHESTER COMMODORE
Courtesy Chicago Defender

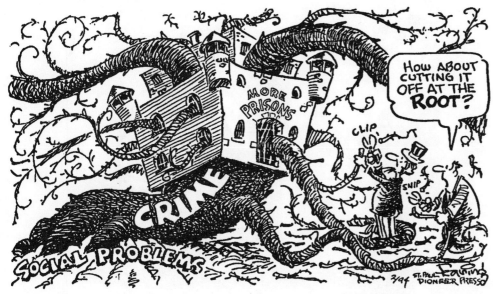

JERRY FEARING
Courtesy St. Paul Pioneer Press-Dispatch

DENNY PRITCHARD
Courtesy Ottawa Citizen

DOUGLAS REGALIA
Courtesy San Ramon Valley Times (Calif.)

JERRY BUCKLEY
Courtesy Express Newspapers

KIRK ANDERSON
Courtesy Madison (Wis.) Capital Times

LARRY WRIGHT
Courtesy Detroit News

CHARLES DANIEL
Courtesy Knoxville News-Sentinel

STEVEN LAIT
Courtesy Oakland Tribune

EDDIE GERMANO
Courtesy The Enterprise (Mass.)

90

Health

As the general public gained a better understanding of just what the sweeping 245-page draft of the Clinton health plan contained, opposition grew in Congress and among voters across the country. The proposed measure soon developed into the No. 1 political issue as President Clinton and Hillary Rodham Clinton tried to rally their forces to save it. Lined up against the bill were the medical profession, the legal profession, drug companies, insurance companies, big business, small business, medium business, and both houses of Congress.

A majority of citizens breathed a collective sigh of relief when the plan finally expired of its own weight. Congress still realizes that reforms need to be made in the nation's health-care system, but few Americans believe that the entire system needs to be overhauled. In any event, it became clear that universal coverage was out.

The Federal Trade Commission, the agency that regulates advertising, decided in June to drop a suit against the R. J. Reynolds Tobacco Company alleging that Reynolds' cartoon figure, Joe Camel, deliberately enticed minors to smoke. Industry leaders were called before Congress to answer charges that they purposely had made cigarettes addictive, but the allegations were not proved.

A study by the Center for Science in the Public Interest showed that seven out of ten movie theaters prepare popcorn in coconut oil. Largely saturated fat, this oil can raise one's cholesterol level.

YOU THOUGHT VINCENT PRICE WAS SCARY?

BILL GARNER
Courtesy Washington Times

MICHAEL RAMIREZ
Courtesy Memphis Commercial Appeal

EUGENE PAYNE
Courtesy Charlotte Observer

JEFF MACNELLY
Courtesy Chicago Tribune and
Tribune Media Services

BOB GORRELL
Courtesy Richmond Times-Dispatch/
Copley News Service

ED STEIN
Courtesy Rocky Mountain News and NEA

MARK CULLUM
Courtesy Birmingham News

WAYNE STAYSKAL
Courtesy Tampa Tribune

KEN CATALINO
Courtesy Anchorage Times

JOHN TREVER
Courtesy Albuquerque Journal

MIKE THOMPSON
Courtesy State Journal-Register (Ill.)

VIC CANTONE
Courtesy Rothco

WAYNE STAYSKAL
Courtesy Tampa Tribune

JIM LANGE
Courtesy Daily Oklahoman

DRAPER HILL
Courtesy Detroit News

SIGNE WILKINSON
Courtesy Philadelphia Daily News

CHRIS OBRION
Courtesy Free Lance-Star (Va.)

NICK ANDERSON
Courtesy Louisville Courier Journal

GARY BROOKINS
Courtesy Richmond Times-Dispatch

JERRY FEARING
Courtesy St. Paul Pioneer Press-Dispatch

"... THIS JUST IN...A THREE-YEAR STUDY SHOWS THAT KNITTING OR READING WHILE DRINKING A CUP OF TEA AND LISTENING TO THE NEWS WITH A CAT CURLED UP ON THE COUCH IS BAD FOR YOU!..."

MIKE LUCKOVICH
Courtesy Atlanta Constitution

GOING IN STYLE...

SCOTT NICKEL
Courtesy Antelope Valley Press (Calif.)

LARRY WRIGHT
Courtesy Detroit News

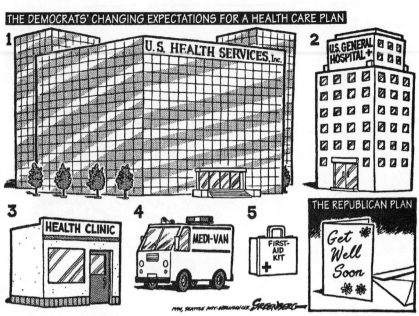

STEVE GREENBERG
Courtesy Seattle Post-Intelligencer

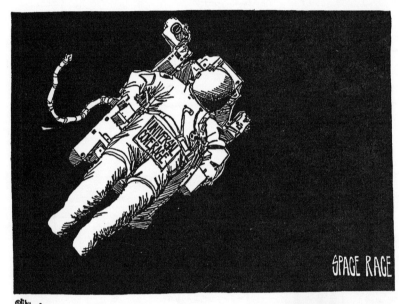

JIM BUSH
Courtesy New Bedford Standard-Times (Mass.)

CHUCK ASAY
Courtesy Colorado Springs Gazette Telegraph

EUGENE PAYNE
Courtesy Charlotte Observer

JOE MAJESKI
Courtesy The Times-Leader (Pa.)

MICKEY SIPORIN
Courtesy Los Angeles Times

ETTA HULME
Courtesy Ft. Worth Star-Telegram

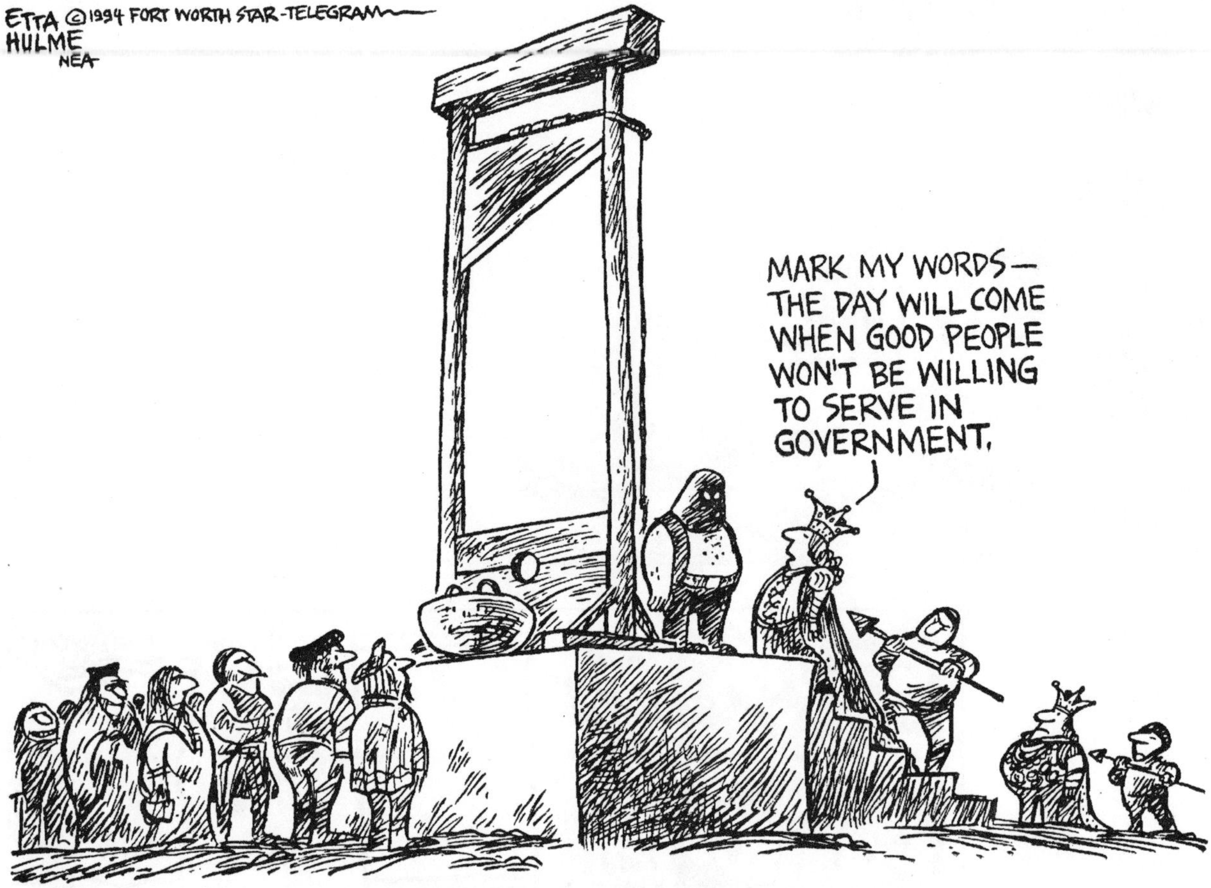
ETTA HULME
©1994 FORT WORTH STAR-TELEGRAM
NEA
MARK MY WORDS—THE DAY WILL COME WHEN GOOD PEOPLE WON'T BE WILLING TO SERVE IN GOVERNMENT.

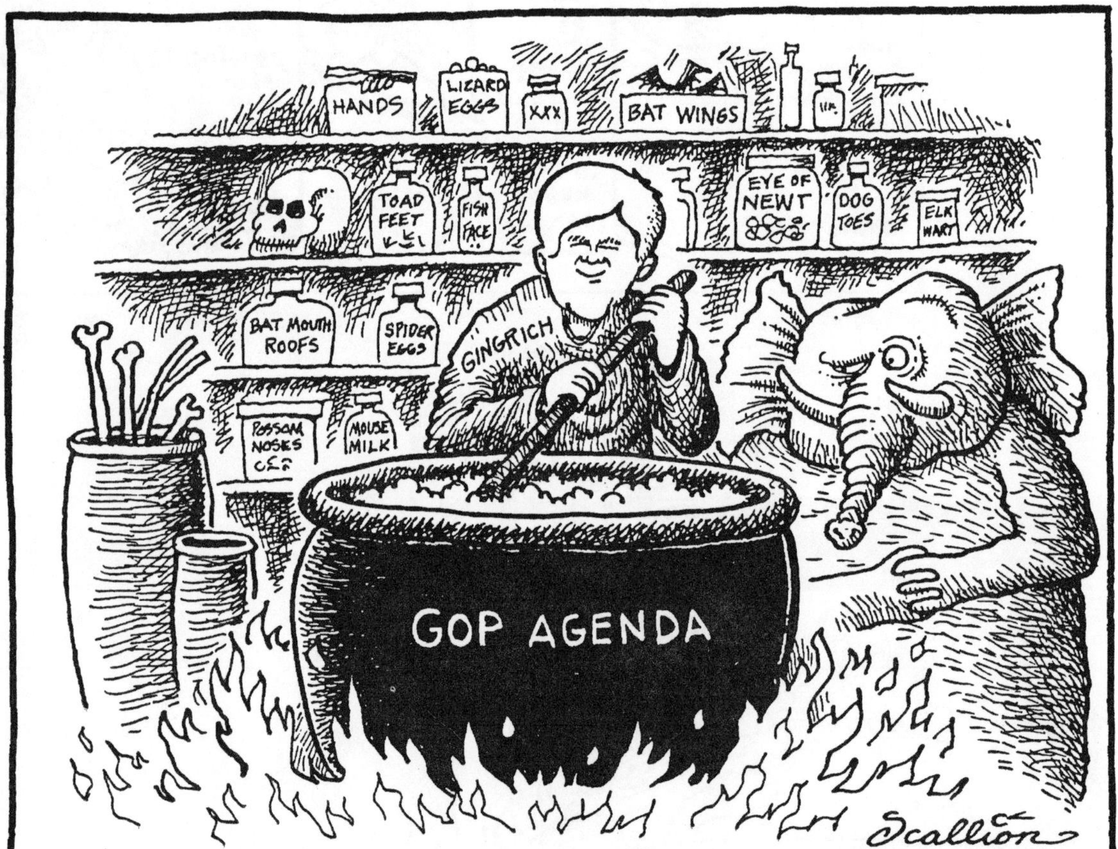
HANDS
LIZARD EGGS
XXX
BAT WINGS
TOAD FEET
FISH FACE
EYE OF NEWT
DOG TOES
ELK WART
BAT MOUTH ROOFS
SPIDER EGGS
GINGRICH
POSSOM NOSES
MOUSE MILK
GOP AGENDA
Scallion
ARK. DEMOCRAT-GAZETTE

STEVE SCALLION
Courtesy Arkansas Democrat-Gazette

Politics

During the fall congressional election campaign, most Democratic incumbents made it clear they did not want to be linked with President Clinton's policies, so the president left the country for the Middle East. Then, citizens across the country voted to turn the Democrats out of office, giving Republicans control of both houses of Congress for the first time in forty years. The election was almost universally viewed as a vote for less government, less spending, and less taxes.

During the campaign, the Republicans announced what they called a Contract with America—a list of ten issues that they promised to bring to a vote in Congress if they won the election. Not a single Republican incumbent was defeated in the November vote.

Rep. Newt Gingrich of Georgia, the new Speaker of the House, rattled liberals when he proposed that orphanages might offer a solution to caring for children living in poverty. When Hillary Clinton attacked the idea, Gingrich recommended that she rent the classic old movie *Boy's Town*, which portrayed Spencer Tracy as Father Flannigan helping orphaned youngsters.

Sen. Jesse Helms created a stir when he told an interviewer that President Clinton was not qualified to be commander-in-chief and that "he'd better have a bodyguard" if he visited military bases in North Carolina.

JEFF MACNELLY
Courtesy Chicago Tribune and
Tribune Media Services

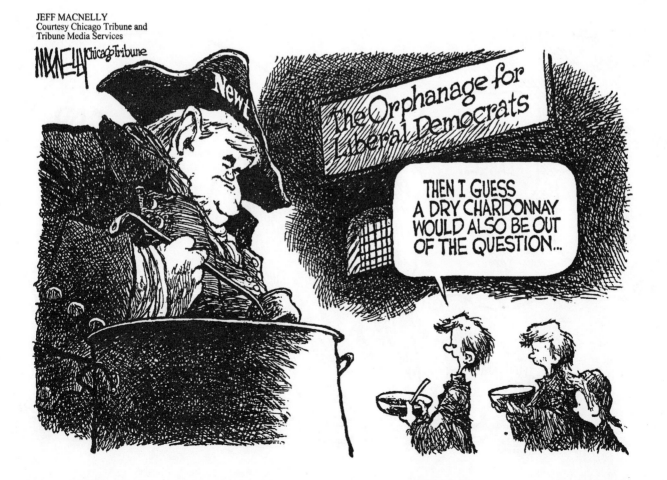

105

JACK MCLEOD
Courtesy Army Times

BRIAN DUFFY
Courtesy Des Moines Register

ETTA HULME
Courtesy Ft. Worth Star-Telegram

106

JEFF MACNELLY
Courtesy Chicago Tribune and
Tribune Media Services

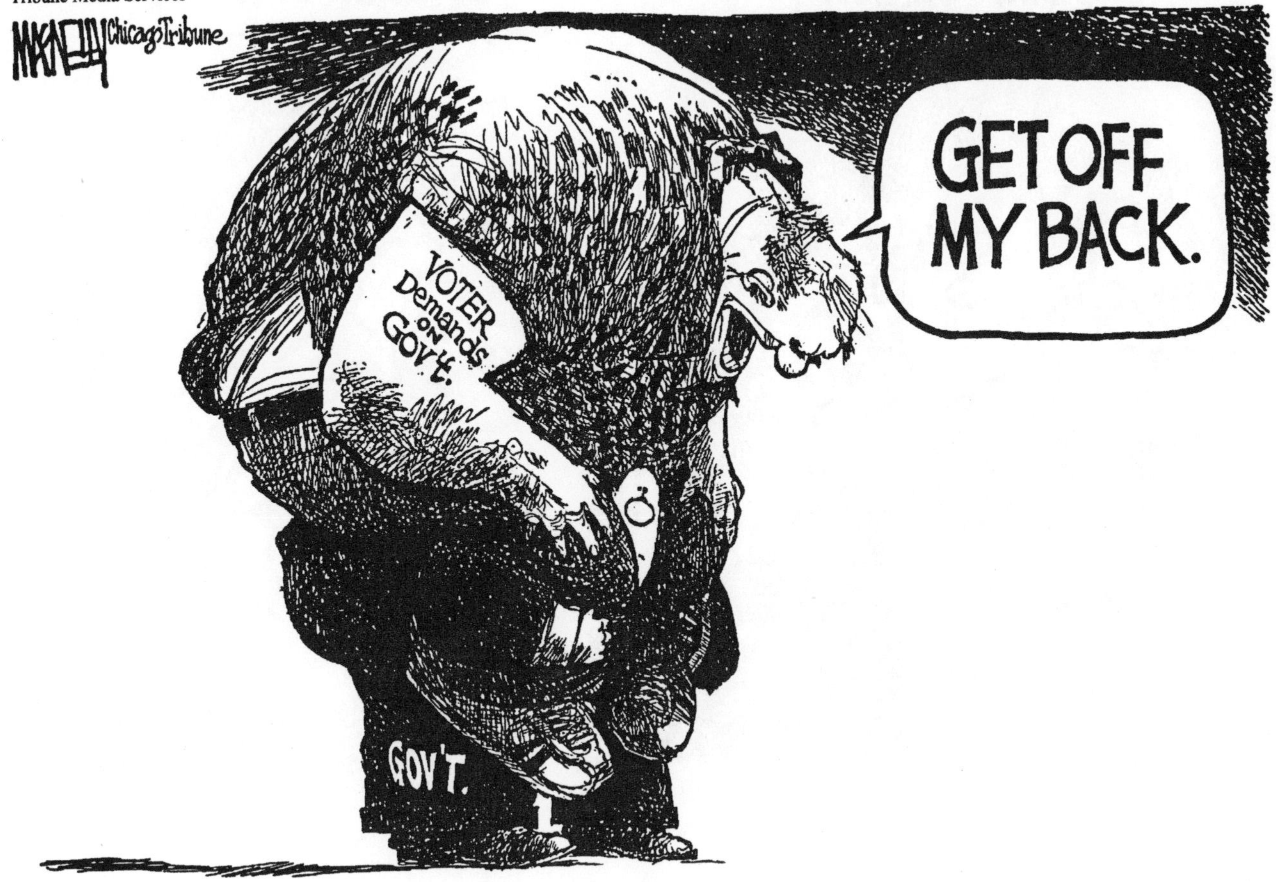
MACNELLY Chicago Tribune
GET OFF MY BACK.
VOTER Demands on Gov't.
GOV'T.

ROB ROGERS
Courtesy Pittsburgh Post-Gazette

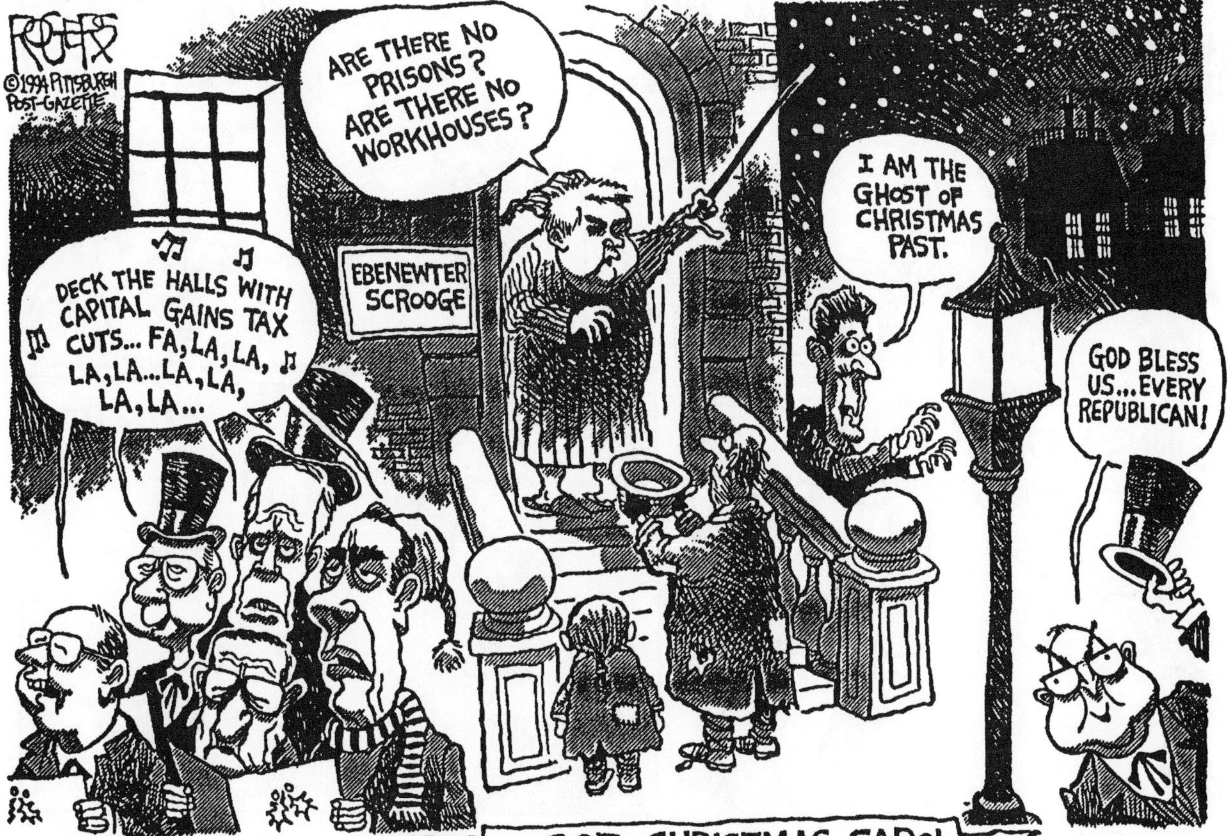
ROGERS ©1994 PITTSBURGH POST-GAZETTE
ARE THERE NO PRISONS? ARE THERE NO WORKHOUSES?
EBENEWTER SCROOGE
I AM THE GHOST OF CHRISTMAS PAST.
DECK THE HALLS WITH CAPITAL GAINS TAX CUTS... FA, LA, LA, LA, LA...LA, LA, LA, LA...
GOD BLESS US...EVERY REPUBLICAN!
A GOP CHRISTMAS CAROL

GUARDING CLINTON

CHAN LOWE
Courtesy The News/Sun-Sentinel (Fla.)

GUARDING JESSE

DANA SUMMERS
Courtesy Orlando Sentinel

JOHN DEERING
Courtesy Arkansas Democrat-Gazette

DICK LOCHER
Courtesy Chicago Tribune

DALE STEPHANOS
Courtesy USA Today

JEFF PARKER
Courtesy Florida Today

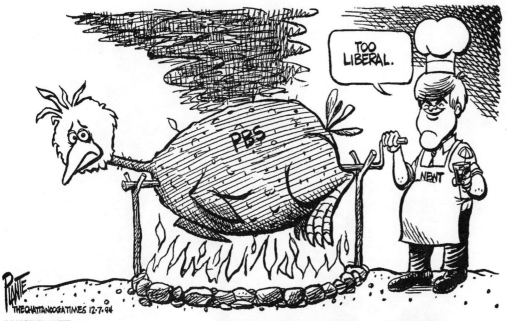

BRUCE PLANTE
Courtesy Chattanooga Times and
Extra Newspapers Features

TOM BECK
Courtesy Freeport Journal-Standard (Ill.)

MILT PRIGGEE
Courtesy Spokane Spokesman-Review

ROGER SCHILLERSTROM
Courtesy Crain Communications

KIRK WALTERS
Courtesy Toledo Blade

The Economy

Major developments on the trade front in 1994 included passage of the North American Free Trade Agreement (NAFTA) and the world-wide General Agreement on Tariffs and Trade (GATT). Each faced substantial opposition but broad bipartisan support carried the day for both. The agreements, intended to lower tariffs throughout the world and encourage free trade, had been sought for years by both Democratic and Republican administrations. Maverick Ross Perot strongly opposed both, maintaining they would cause a massive loss of jobs in the U.S.

Federal Reserve Board chairman Alan Greenspan was repeatedly accused of worrying too much about inflation as he raised short-term interest rates six times during the year. The net result was a modest inflation rate of 2.7 percent for the year. The U.S. economy was estimated to have grown 4.1 percent.

Japan's economy contracted unexpectedly in 1994, hampering the Clinton administration's efforts to open Japan to American goods and services.

Late in the year the Postal Rate Commission announced a three-cent increase in the price of a first-class stamp to thirty-two cents, effective January 1.

SANDY CAMPBELL
Courtesy The Tennessean

GLENN MCCOY
Courtesy Belleville News-Democrat (Ill.)

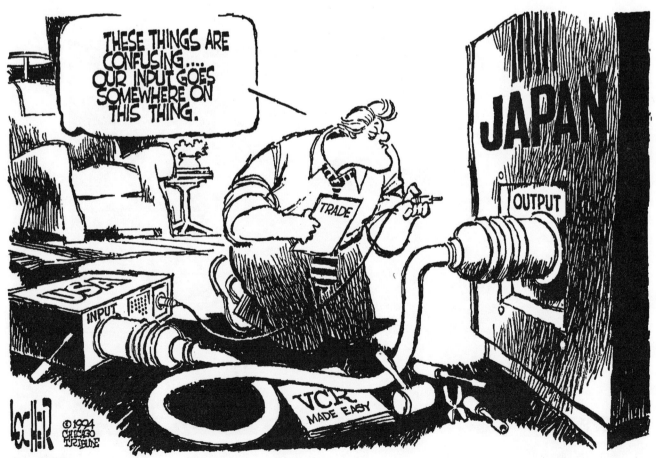

DICK LOCHER
Courtesy Chicago Tribune

MIKE SMITH
Courtesy Las Vegas Sun

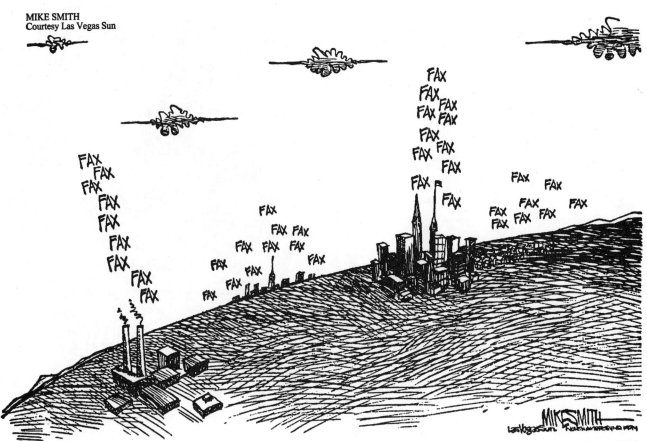

ALL ACROSS THE COUNTRY YOU CAN HEAR THE SOUND OF OUTRAGE AT ANOTHER POSTAL RATE INCREASE.

JACK OHMAN
Courtesy Portland Oregonian

JUST WHAT IS **GATT**, ANYWAY?

IT'S THE PAST TENSE OF "GIT."

YOU'VE OVERLOOKED KIWI IMPORT QUOTAS !!!

AND YOU'VE AVOIDED THE TUNGSTEN STEEL PROVISO !!!

THE GATT? RIGHT NEXT TO THE CARBURETOR...

GENERAL AGREEMENT ON TARIFFS AND TRADE... A BUNCH OF GENERALS AGREED ON SOMETHING...

...JUST ANOTHER EXCUSE TO ROLL OUT THE OL' CHARTS, PEOPLE!!!

DICK WALLMEYER
Courtesy Long Beach Press-Telegram

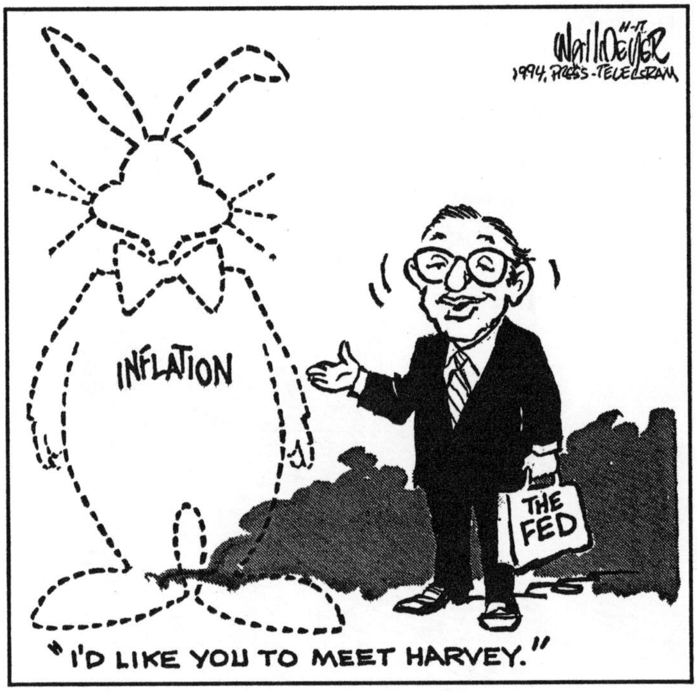
INFLATION
THE FED
"I'D LIKE YOU TO MEET HARVEY."

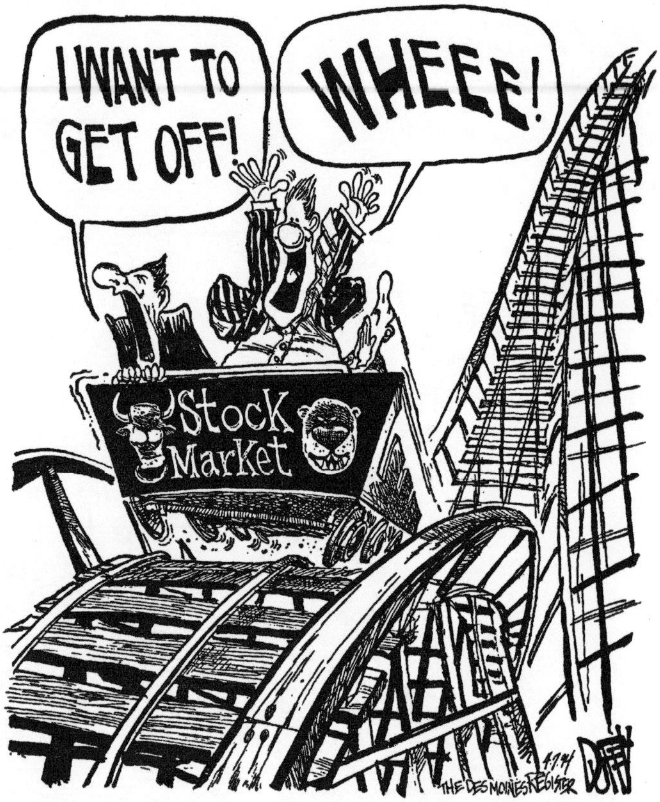
I WANT TO GET OFF!
WHEEE!
Stock Market

BRIAN DUFFY
Courtesy Des Moines Register

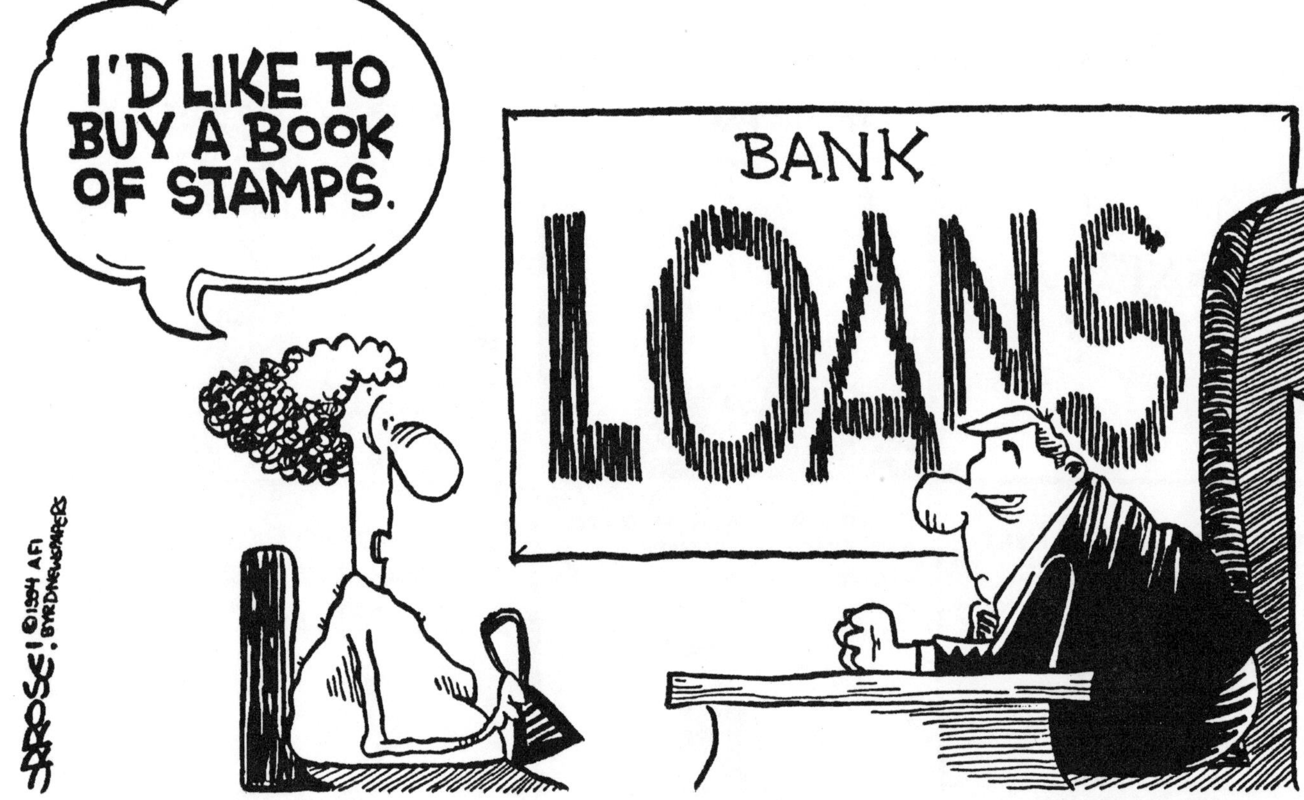
I'D LIKE TO BUY A BOOK OF STAMPS.
BANK
LOANS

J. R. ROSE
Courtesy Byrd Newspapers

WES RAND
Courtesy Norwich Bulletin

JEFF DANZIGER
Courtesy Christian Science Monitor

JOHN SPENCER
Courtesy Philadelphia Business Journal

TOM BECK
Courtesy Freeport Journal-Standard (Ill.)

BOB GORRELL
Courtesy Richmond Times-Dispatch/
Copley News Service

DAVE COVERLY
Courtesy Bloomington Herald-Times

DON LEE
Courtesy Sandusky Register

ETTA HULME
Courtesy Ft. Worth Star-Telegram

LARRY WRIGHT
Courtesy Detroit News

ED FISCHER
Courtesy Rochester Post-Bulletin

WAYNE STAYSKAL
Courtesy Tampa Tribune

KIRK ANDERSON
Courtesy Madison (Wis.) Capital Times

DANA SUMMERS
Courtesy Orlando Sentinel

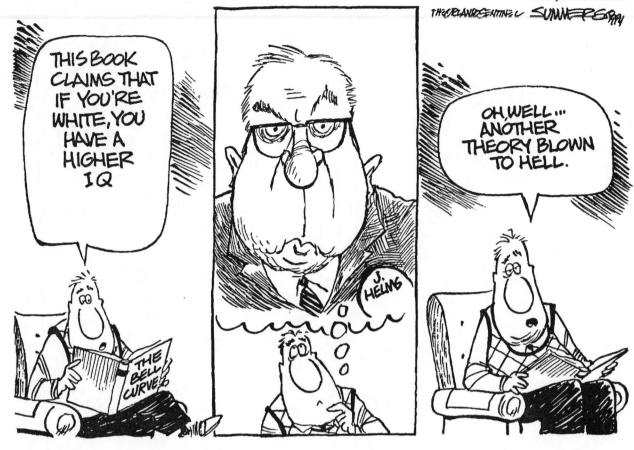

NEIL GRAHAME
Courtesy Spencer Newspapers

Congress

Longtime congressman Dan Rostenkowski of Illinois, one of the most powerful political figures on Capitol Hill, was rocked during the year with a seventeen-count indictment. The charges against him ranged from converting postage stamps into cash, to hiring "ghost employees" who did little or no work for hefty salaries, to taking unlawful privileges during his thirty-five years as a congressman. He surrendered his post as chairman of the House Ways and Means Committee and later was defeated for reelection.

President Clinton pushed through a limited crime bill that critics panned as just another social program by the Democrats.

Sen. Jesse Helms made headlines once again. He told a television interviewer that President Clinton was not qualified to be commander-in-chief of the military, and that if he visits military bases in North Carolina, "he'd better have a bodyguard." The media had a field day with the ill-conceived remark and Helms later apologized. Senator Helms was in line to assume one of the most prestigious jobs in government—chairmanship of the Senate Foreign Relations Committee

WALT HANDELSMAN
Courtesy Times-Picayune (N.O.)

123

CHARLES BISSELL
Courtesy The Tennessean

DAVID DONAR
Courtesy Macomb Daily (Miss.)

JACK HIGGINS
Courtesy Chicago Sun-Times

124

JEFF DANZIGER
Courtesy Christian Science Monitor

BOB RICH
Courtesy Connecticut Post

Berry's World

JIM BERRY
Courtesy NEA

And NOW!

ART WOOD
Courtesy Farm Bureau News

DICK WALLMEYER
Courtesy Long Beach Press-Telegram

ROSTENKOWSKI COMES OUT FIGHTING

JACK MCLEOD
Courtesy Army Times

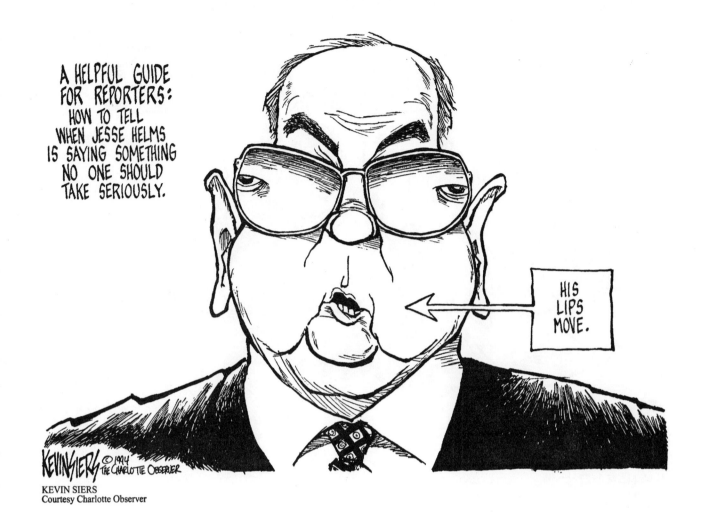

KEVIN SIERS
Courtesy Charlotte Observer

MIKE SMITH
Courtesy Las Vegas Sun

ART HENRIKSON
Courtesy Daily Herald (Ill.)

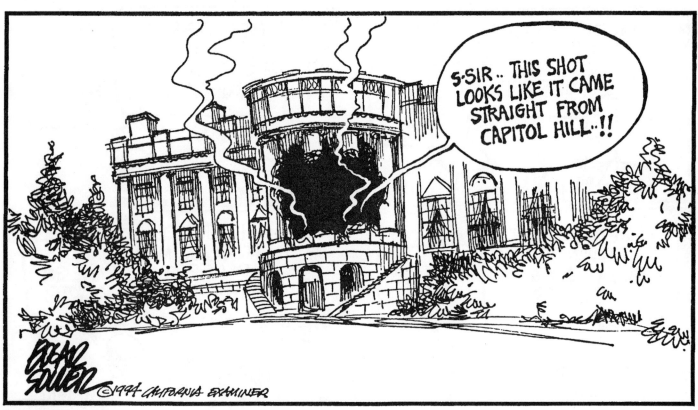

EDGAR SOLLER
Courtesy California Examiner

The Family and Society

Pope John Paul II issued a stern letter to Catholic bishops in 1994 reaffirming the church's ban on women priests. It was not a popular message, particularly in view of the fact that the Roman Catholic church faces a critical shortage of priests. Critics noted that two years earlier the Church of England had begun to ordain women as priests. The pope also stood fast in opposition to abortion.

Abortion clinics in several states were targeted by pro-life advocates for anti-abortion protests. Some of the protests escalated into violence, resulting in the murder of a Florida abortionist and his aide and two receptionists at a clinic in Boston.

Gang membership continued to grow during the year. Census Bureau statistics showed that 34 percent of the nation's 65.7 million children under the age of eighteen do not grow up in "traditional families," that is, with both a father and a mother present. Instead, many are reared in one-parent homes, blended families, or on the streets. Many states have enacted laws to help pursue runaway and deadbeat fathers in an effort to force them to assume responsibility for their families.

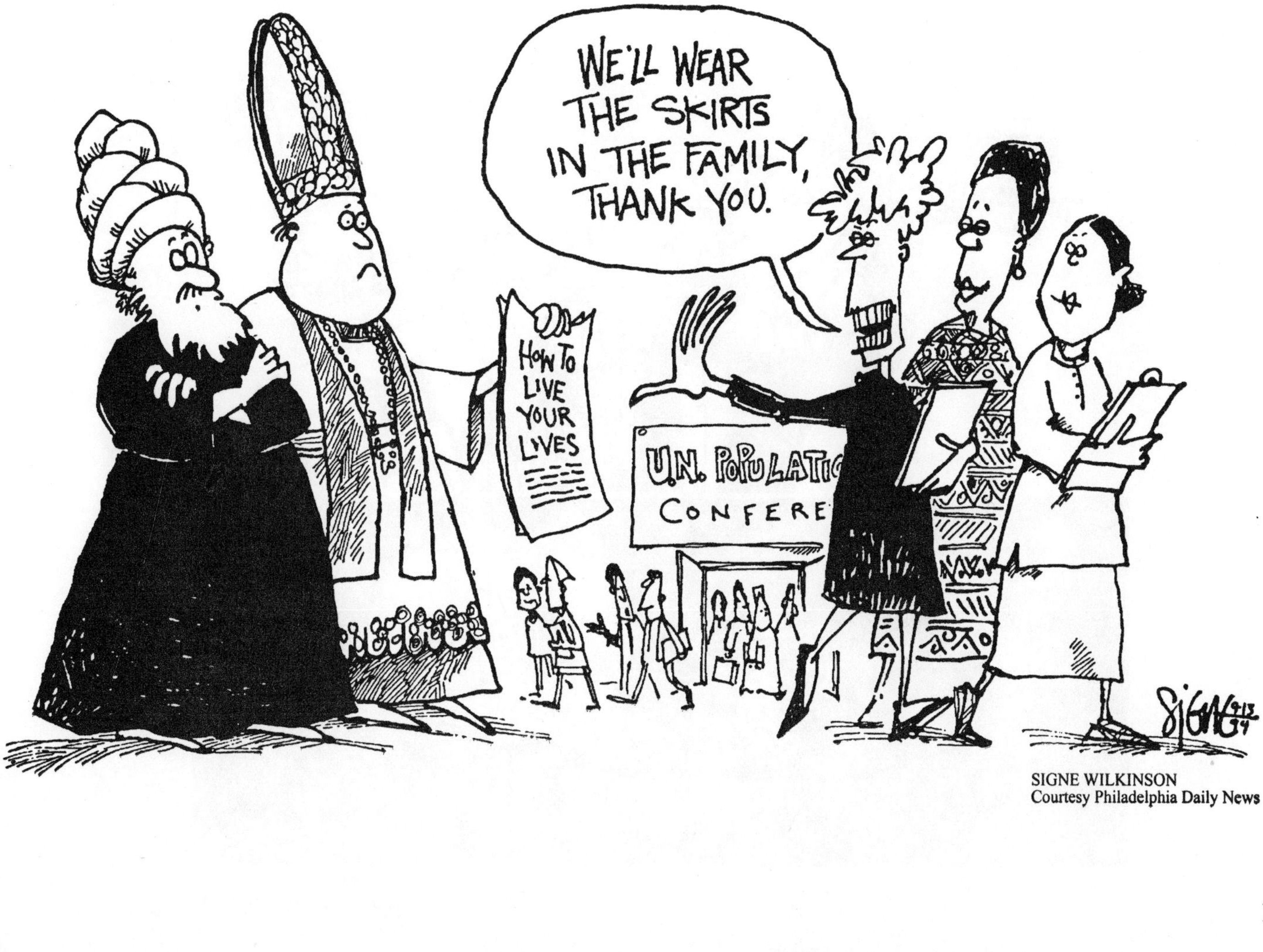
WE'LL WEAR THE SKIRTS IN THE FAMILY, THANK YOU.
HOW TO LIVE YOUR LIVES
U.N. POPULATI
CONFERE
SIGNE

SIGNE WILKINSON
Courtesy Philadelphia Daily News

DAVID HITCH
Courtesy Worcester Telegram & Gazette

JIM MCCLOSKEY
Courtesy Staunton Daily News Leader

MIKE LUCKOVICH
Courtesy Atlanta Constitution

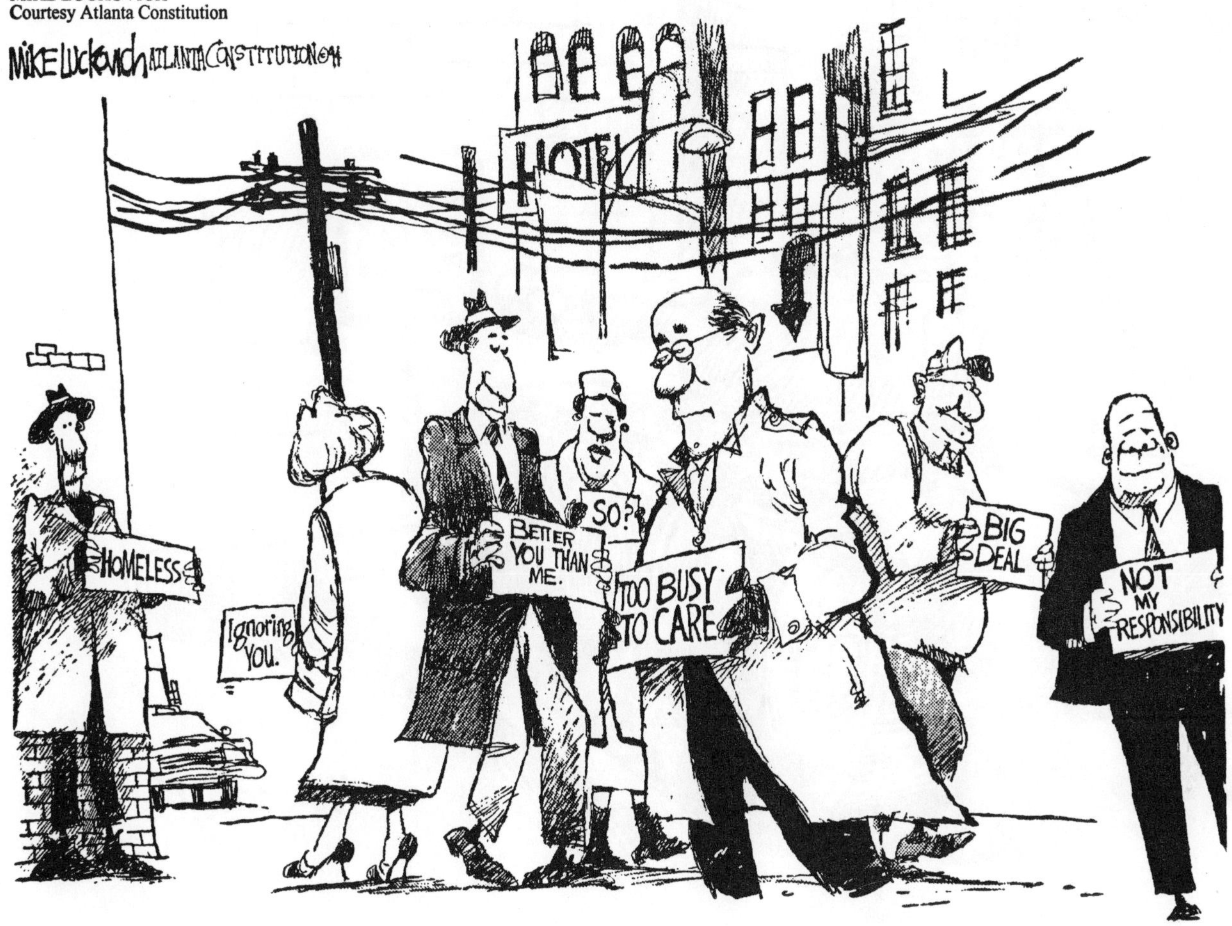
MIKE LUCKOVICH ATLANTA CONSTITUTION ©94
HOTEL
HOMELESS
Ignoring You.
BETTER YOU THAN ME.
SO?
TOO BUSY TO CARE
BIG DEAL
NOT MY RESPONSIBILITY

MICHAEL RAMIREZ
Courtesy Memphis Commercial Appeal

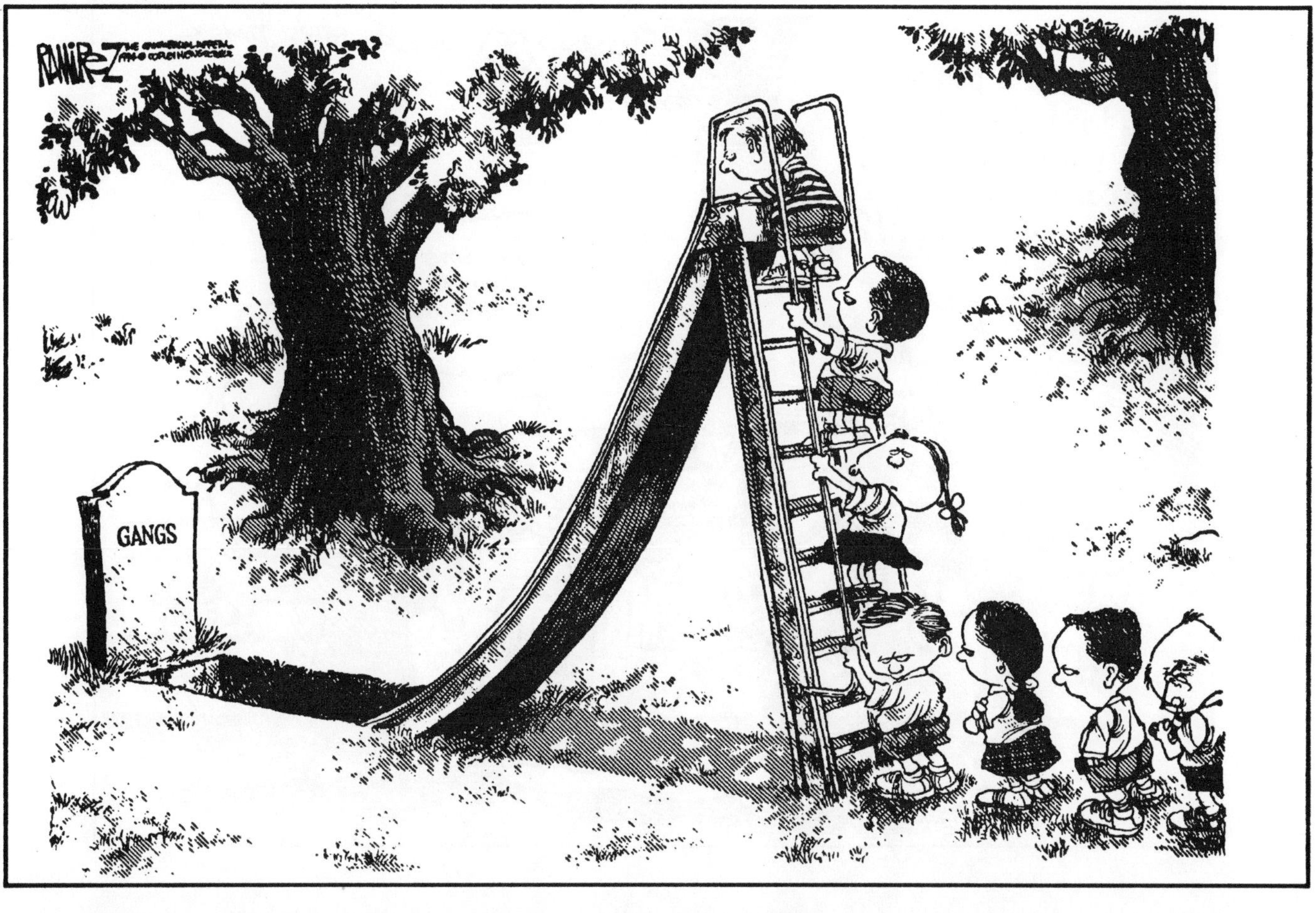
RAMIREZ
GANGS

MARGULIES
©1994 THE RECORD
NEW JERSEY

JIMMY MARGULIES
Courtesy The Record (N.J.)/
North American Syndicate

DOUGLAS REGALIA
Courtesy San Ramon Valley Times (Calif.)

"TEN YEARS AGO, IF WE'D SENT A KID TO SCHOOL LOOKING LIKE THAT, THEY'D HAVE CHARGED US WITH CHILD ABUSE!"

MICHAEL GILLETT
Courtesy Portsmouth Daily Times (Ohio)

JAMES GRASDAL
Courtesy Edmonton Journal

JEFF STAHLER
Courtesy Cincinnati Post

BOB DORNFRIED
Courtesy Fairfield Citizen-News (Conn.)

DAVID HITCH
Courtesy Worcester Telegram & Gazette

GREG HORVAY
Courtesy Philadelphia Daily News

CHARLES FAGAN
Courtesy Associated Features Syndicate

CHAN LOWE
Courtesy The News/Sun-Sentinel (Fla.)

MALCOLM MAYES
Courtesy Edmonton Journal

JOHN DEERING
Courtesy Arkansas Democrat-Gazette

JEFF MACNELLY
Courtesy Chicago Tribune and
Tribune Media Services

Jimmy Carter

Former president Jimmy Carter held the world spotlight during 1994. Because of inaction on the part of the Clinton administration, diplomatic relations between the U.S. and North Korea were deteriorating rapidly by the middle of the year. It was suspected that Pyongyang was building a nuclear weapons program, and the outlaw nation refused to allow a United Nations inspection team to visit the sites in question. Two graphite nuclear reactors that could produce about 350 pounds of weapons-grade plutonium per year were under construction. As the two countries edged toward a possible military showdown, Carter came to Clinton's rescue. The former president at least temporarily defused the issue and brokered an agreement for the first summit meeting between North and South Korean leaders since World War II. Some observers speculated that he might have promised too much in order to finalize the agreement.

Near the end of the summer, the Clinton administration threatened to invade Haiti unless its military leaders stepped down and allowed ousted president Jean-Bertrand Aristide to return to power. With an invasion imminent, last-minute discussions with Carter, Sen. Sam Nunn, and Gen. Colin Powell persuaded the military junta to quit. American troops landed peacefully, Aristide returned to power, and Carter turned his attention to the war in Bosnia.

JEFF KOTERBA
Courtesy Omaha World-Herald

GLENN MCCOY
Courtesy Belleville News-Democrat (Ill.)

DICK LOCHER
Courtesy Chicago Tribune

NICK ANDERSON
Courtesy Louisville Courier Journal

PATRICK RICE
Courtesy Jupiter Courier

GEORGE DANBY
Courtesy Bangor Daily News

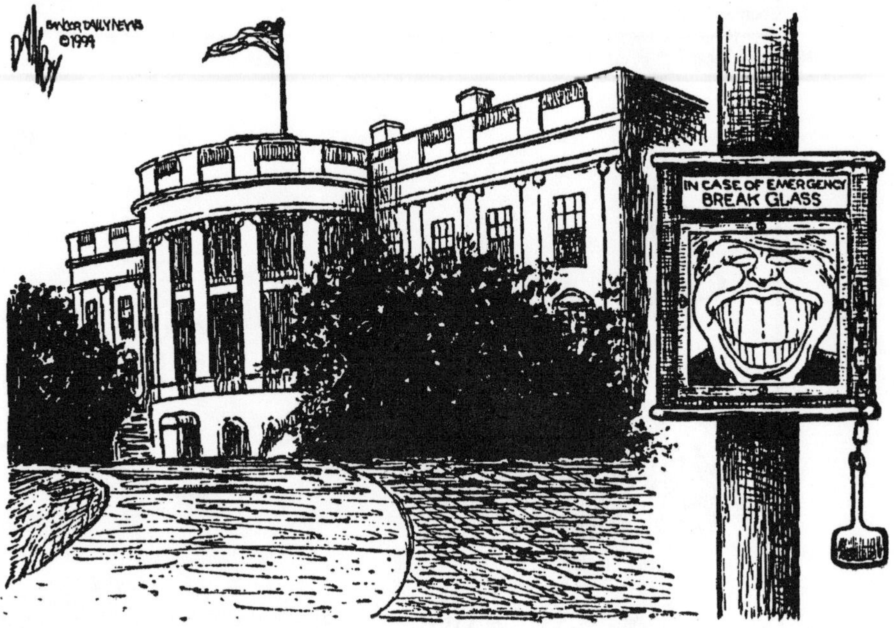
BANGOR DAILY NEWS ©1994
IN CASE OF EMERGENCY
BREAK GLASS

GARY BROOKINS
Courtesy Richmond Times-Dispatch

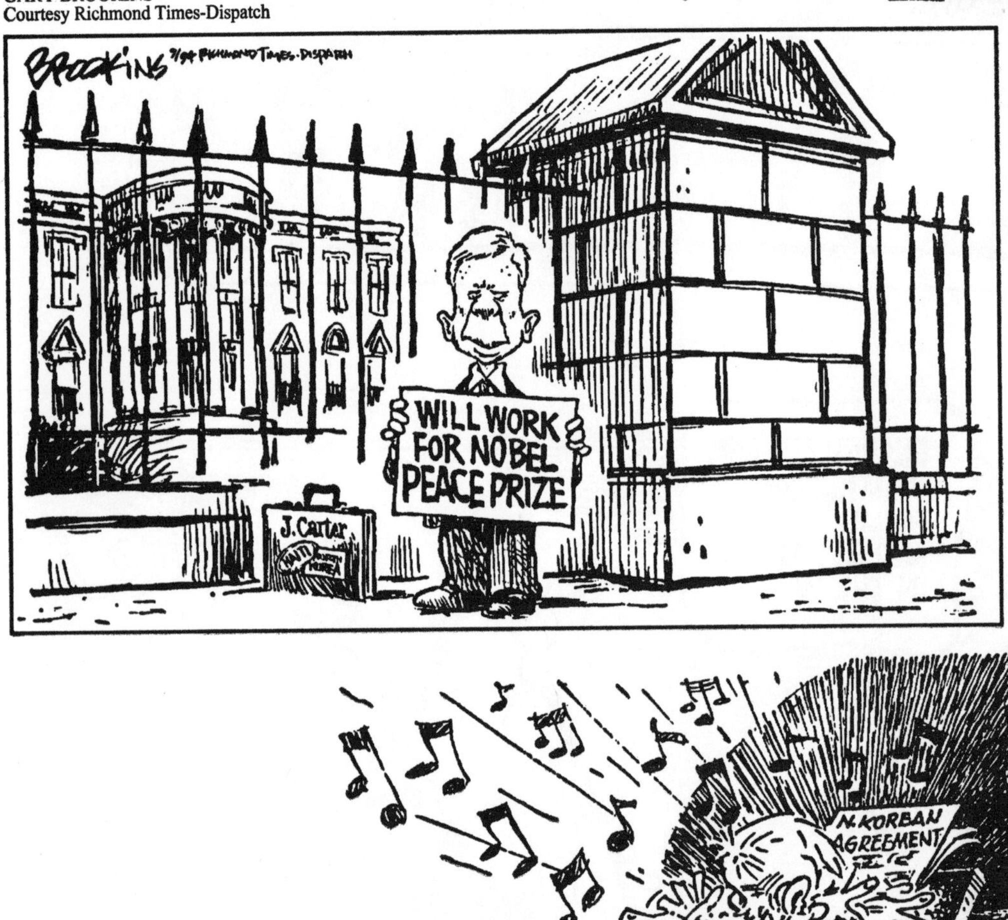
BROOKINS
WILL WORK FOR NOBEL PEACE PRIZE
J. Carter

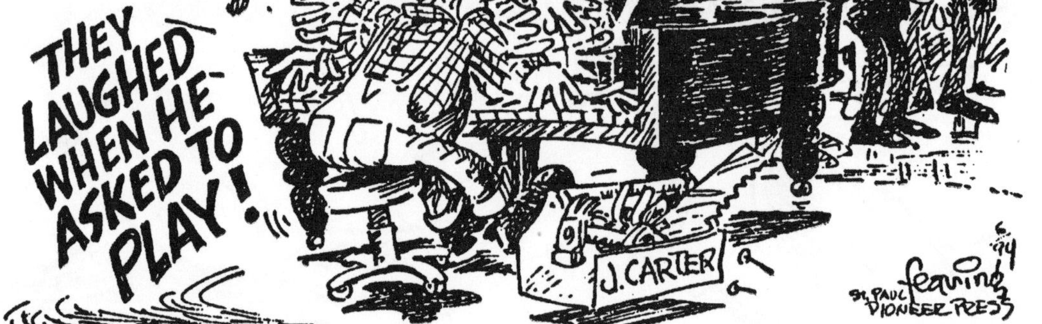
N. KOREAN AGREEMENT
THEY LAUGHED WHEN HE ASKED TO PLAY!
J. CARTER
ST. PAUL PIONEER PRESS

JERRY FEARING
Courtesy St. Paul Pioneer Press-Dispatch

DAVE COVERLY
Courtesy Bloomington Herald-Times

JEFF PARKER
Courtesy Florida Today

MARK STREETER
Courtesy Savannah Morning News

JOEL PETT
Courtesy Lexington Herald-Leader

The Middle East

Following a historic Israeli-Arab peace agreement, Palestinian leader Yasser Arafat returned to Jerusalem in July for the first time since 1967 when Israel seized the Arab part of the city. Israel and Jordan also agreed to end forty-six years of hostility. Opposing the peace moves, Hezbollah and Hamas zealots vowed to renew terrorist attacks in an effort to sabotage the agreement. As the year ended, extremists on both sides were still fighting sporadically.

Late in the year, Iraq's Saddam Hussein moved two divisions of his Republican Guard toward the Kuwait border. President Clinton reacted quickly, ordering the aircraft carrier *George Washington* and other forces into the Persian Gulf region. Arab and European leaders signaled their support for Clinton's moves, and Saddam's troops were soon withdrawn.

Analysts suspected that the ploy by Iraq was a weak effort to intimidate the United Nations into lifting sanctions that have shackled the nation's economy.

DICK LOCHER
Courtesy Chicago Tribune

"Take me to Stockholm for the Nobel Peace Prize ceremony..."

JIMMY MARGULIES
Courtesy The Record (N.J.)/
North American Syndicate

STEVE BREEN
Courtesy Asbury Park Press (N.J.)

THE PIECE PROCESS

NEAL BLOOM
Courtesy Jewish Cartoon Productions

NEAL BLOOM
Courtesy Jewish Cartoon Productions

HANK MCCLURE
Courtesy Lawton Constitution

LAMBERT DER
Courtesy Houston Post

CHAN LOWE
Courtesy The News/Sun-Sentinel (Fla.)

GILL FOX
Courtesy Connecticut Post

FRANK CAMMUSO
Courtesy Syracuse Herald-Journal

THE MOTHER of ALL LEFTOVERS

MILT PRIGGEE
Courtesy Spokane Spokesman-Review

MILT PRIGGEE
Courtesy Spokane Spokesman-Review

DAVID HORSEY
Courtesy Seattle Post-Intelligencer

Education

A study by the government's National Assessment of Educational Progress determined that there has been some small improvement in the level of student learning in mathematics and science since 1983, but also concluded that there has been no increase in reading and writing skills. Approximately half of the youngsters in public school do not graduate from high school, and about half of those who do cannot read as well as they should. Republicans have targeted education as one of the areas in which they intend to focus a major effort for improvement.

The battle over prayer in school, or the lack of it, continued during the year, but a definitive ruling on the matter was nowhere in sight.

Since the mid-1980s, juvenile violence has grown much faster than the juvenile population and arrests of youth under the age of eighteen for murder have more than doubled. This trend is being reflected in schools as more and more weapons are being brought in—and sometimes confiscated—daily. School arguments that once were settled with fists are now often addressed with guns.

MIKE LUCKOVICH
Courtesy Atlanta Constitution

ROB ROGERS
Courtesy Pittsburgh Post-Gazette

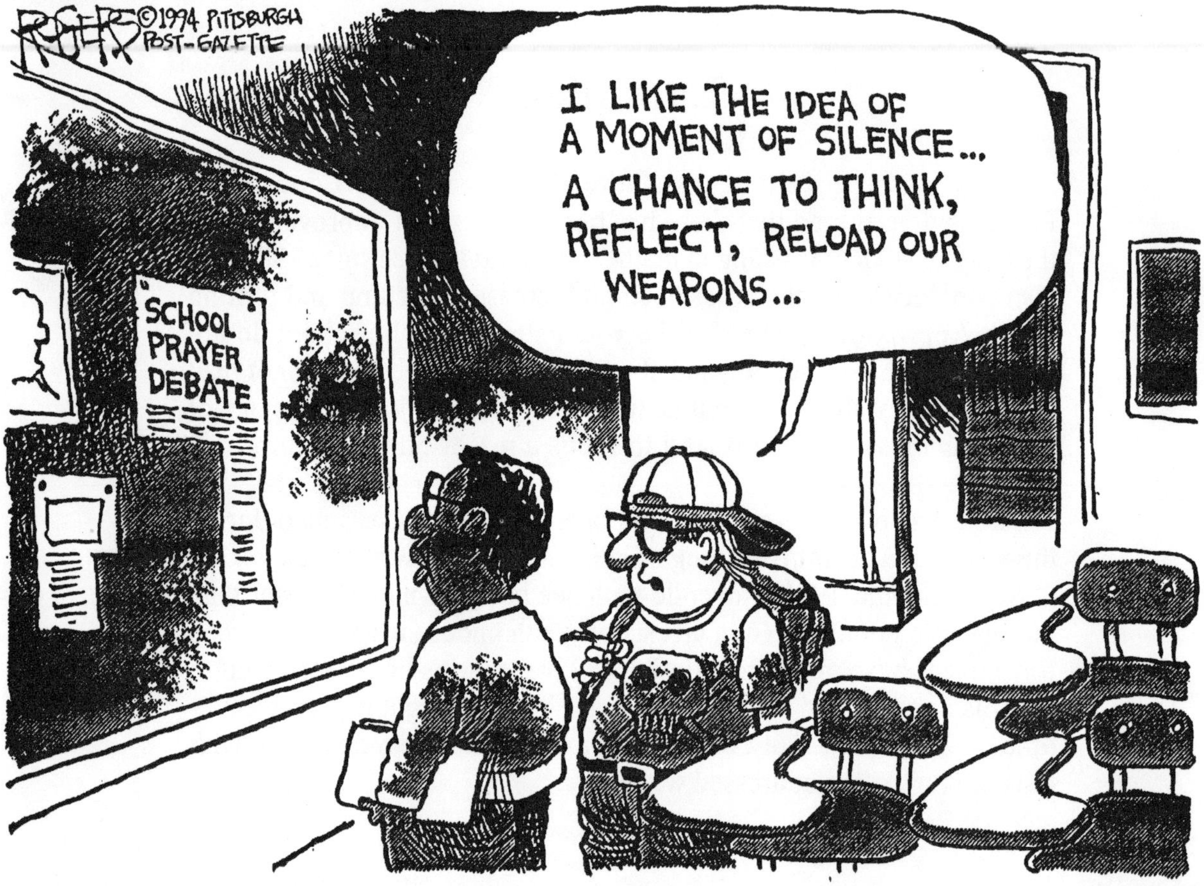
ROGERS ©1994 PITTSBURGH POST-GAZETTE
I LIKE THE IDEA OF A MOMENT OF SILENCE... A CHANCE TO THINK, REFLECT, RELOAD OUR WEAPONS...
SCHOOL PRAYER DEBATE

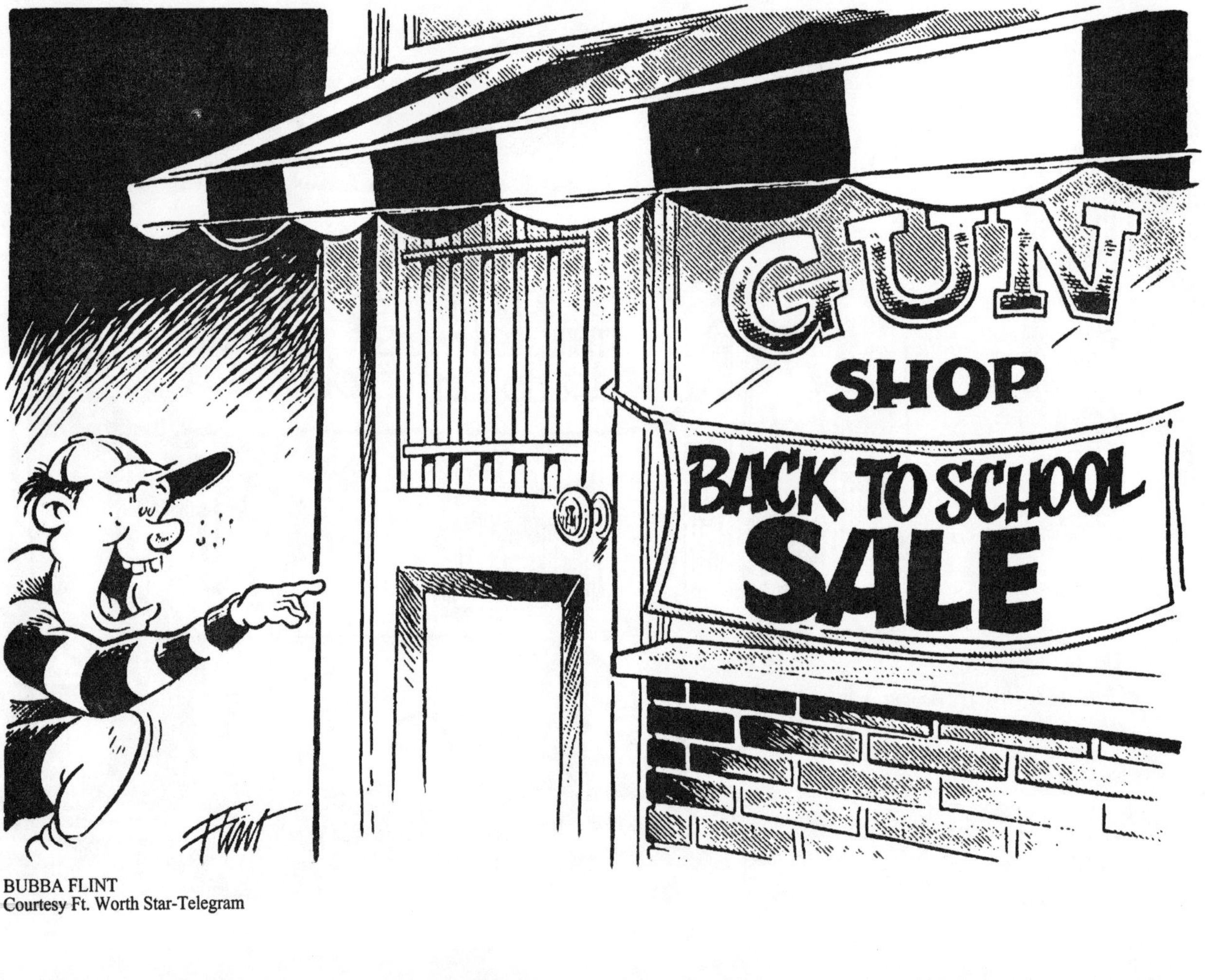
GUN
SHOP
BACK TO SCHOOL
SALE
Flint

BUBBA FLINT
Courtesy Ft. Worth Star-Telegram

MICHAEL RAMIREZ
Courtesy Memphis Commercial Appeal

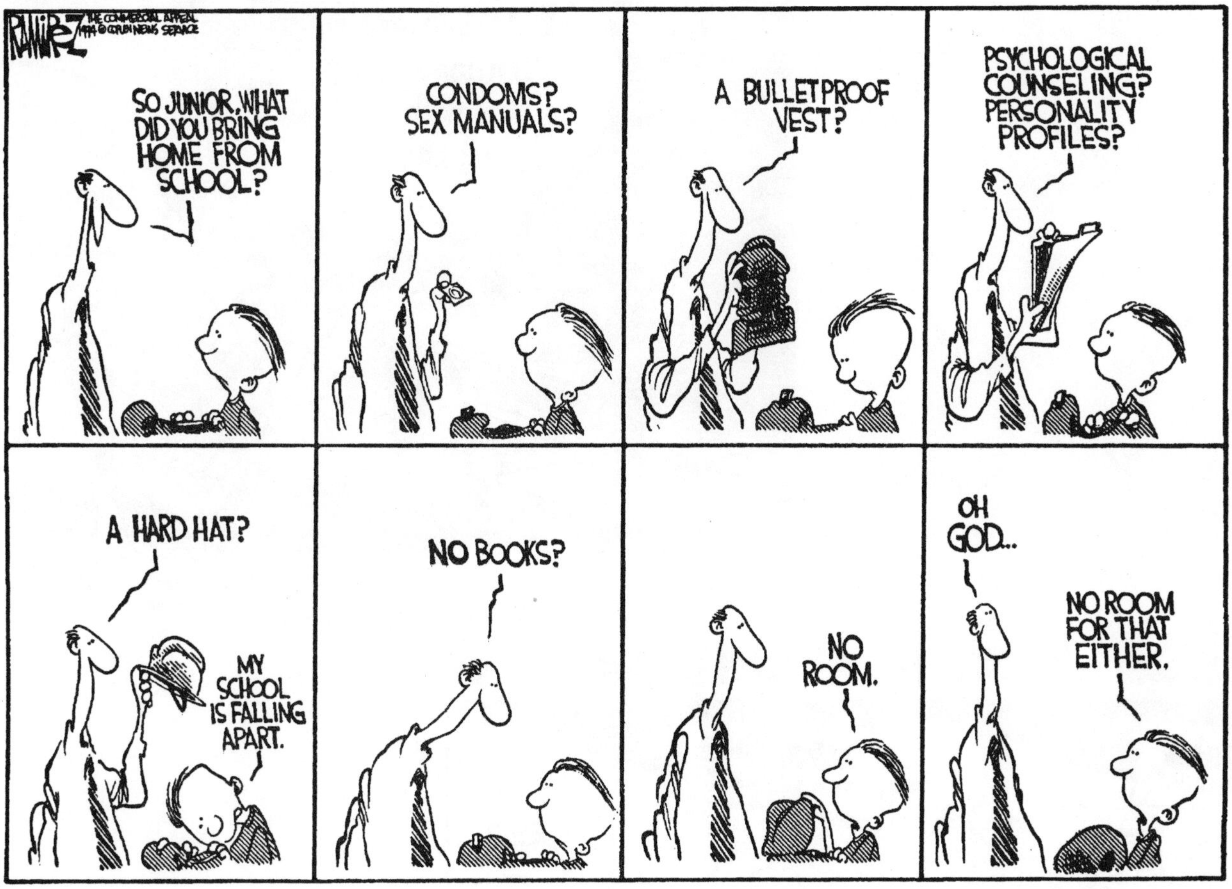
RAMIREZ THE COMMERCIAL APPEAL 1994 © COPLEY NEWS SERVICE
SO JUNIOR, WHAT DID YOU BRING HOME FROM SCHOOL?
CONDOMS? SEX MANUALS?
A BULLETPROOF VEST?
PSYCHOLOGICAL COUNSELING? PERSONALITY PROFILES?
A HARD HAT?
MY SCHOOL IS FALLING APART.
NO BOOKS?
NO ROOM.
OH GOD..
NO ROOM FOR THAT EITHER.

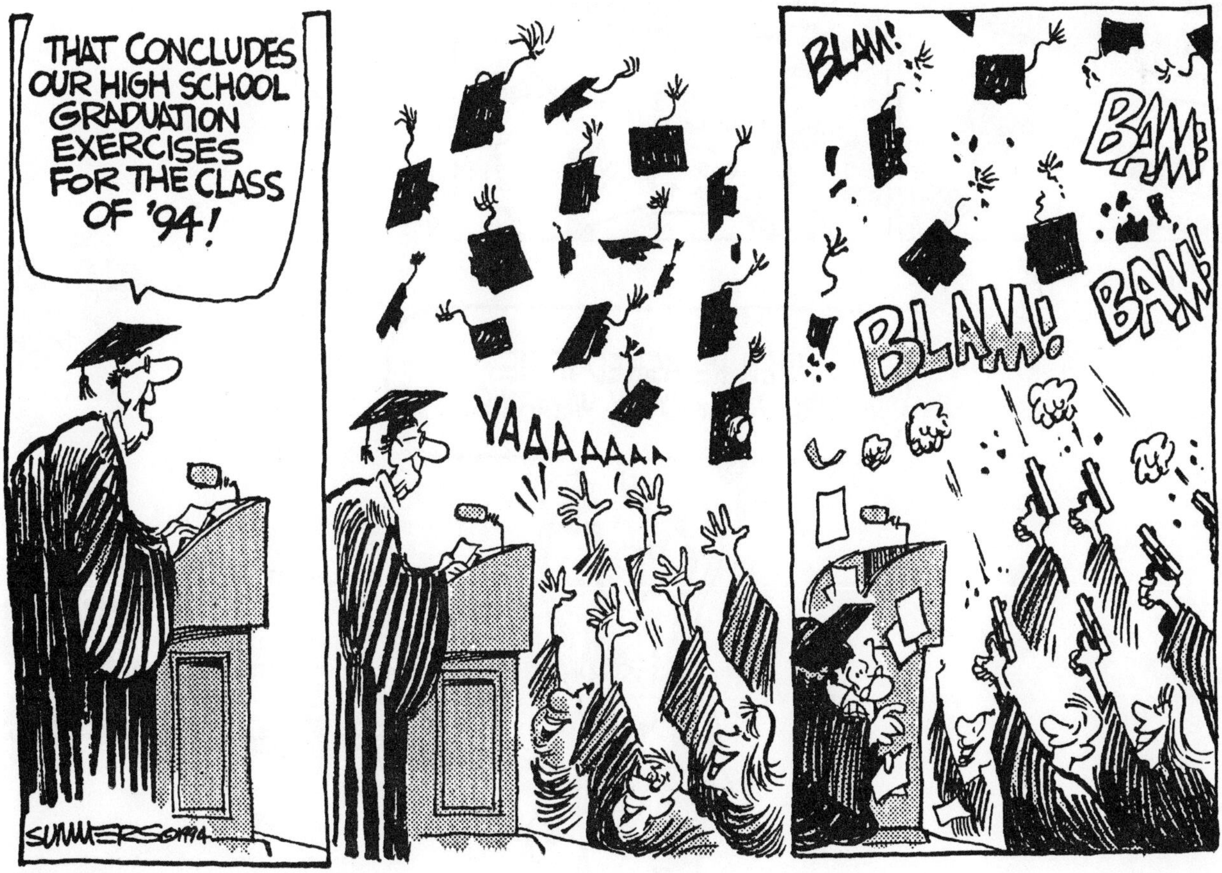
THAT CONCLUDES OUR HIGH SCHOOL GRADUATION EXERCISES FOR THE CLASS OF '94!
YAAAAAAA
BLAM!
BAM!
BAM!
BLAM!
SUMMERS ©1994

DANA SUMMERS
Courtesy Orlando Sentinel

MARSHALL RAMSEY
Courtesy Conroe Courier (Tex.)

SCOTT BATEMAN
Courtesy Baker City Herald (Oreg.)

JEFF STAHLER
Courtesy Cincinnati Post

SANDY CAMPBELL
Courtesy The Tennessean

REX BABIN
Courtesy Times Union (N.Y.)

PRAYER IN SCHOOL

MICHAEL RAMIREZ
Courtesy Memphis Commercial Appeal

ROY PETERSON
Courtesy Vancouver Sun

Immigration

The wave of refugees from Haiti and Cuba attempting to enter the United States continued in 1994. During the early part of the year, the U.S. Coast Guard intercepted scores of boats jammed with people fleeing their impoverished and repressive homelands. Under a new policy adopted June 16, refugees apprehended on the high seas were given a hearing to determine if they qualified for refugee status.

After the U.S. peaceably invaded Haiti in late September, the flow of refugees from that beleaguered country ceased. U.S. troops and Haitian police patrolled the beaches to ensure that there was no new exodus northward.

In September, an agreement was reached with Cuba that should stem the tide of refugees from that troubled Communist country. The agreement called for the U.S. to admit at least 20,000 Cubans a year.

In November, voters in California approved the controversial Proposition 187, which denies illegal immigrants the generous education and health-care benefits currently provided by the state's taxpayers. The proposition was immediately challenged in court, however, and by year's end had not been implemented.

GARY BROOKINS
Courtesy Richmond Times-Dispatch

BAY OF PIGS INVASION...CUBAN STYLE!

LAZARO FRESQUET
Courtesy El Nuevo Herald (Miami)

RICK KOLLINGER
Courtesy Easton Star Democrat (Md.)

LAZARO FRESQUET
Courtesy El Nuevo Herald (Miami)

MATT WUERKER
Courtesy The Easy Reader

JACK HIGGINS
Courtesy Chicago Sun-Times

The Simpson Case

A nation that had become virtually immune to being shocked by violence was thunderstruck in June when a well-known and widely respected celebrity was accused of a double murder. Nicole Brown Simpson, the ex-wife of former football great, movie star, and television pitchman O. J. Simpson, and her friend, Ronald Goldman, were brutally butchered outside her front door, and evidence seemed to point to her famed ex-husband.

After being arrested and charged with the crime, Simpson hired one of the nation's most acclaimed trial lawyers, Robert Shapiro, to head a team of attorneys to defend him in court. The pretrial hearings immediately took on the appearance of a circus. Under the glaring lights of television, media coverage soon surpassed that of any previous court case in history. Just about every person even remotely associated with the case was sought for interviews by the press, and the gory details of the crime scene were rehashed extensively by the media.

Jury selection proved to be difficult because of the extensive public attention on the case. After the jurors were seated, presiding judge Lance Ito barred them from access to radio, television, newspapers, and magazines unless censored. The trial was scheduled to begin in late January.

DICK WRIGHT
Courtesy Providence Journal-Bulletin

RICHARD CROWSON
Courtesy Wichita Eagle

ROB ROGERS
Courtesy Pittsburgh Post-Gazette

JOHN MARSHALL
Courtesy Binghampton Press and Sun Bulletin

JEFF KOTERBA
Courtesy Omaha World-Herald

BRUCE MACKINNON
Courtesy Halifax Chronicle-Herald

GARY BROOKINS
Courtesy Richmond Times-Dispatch

WALT HANDELSMAN
Courtesy Times-Picayune (N.O.)

STEVE SACK
Courtesy Minneapolis Star-Tribune

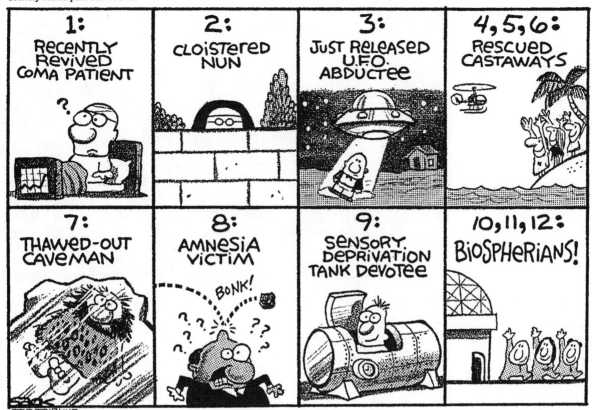

ASSEMBLING AN UNBIASED O.J. SIMPSON JURY....

DALE STEPHANOS
Courtesy Boston Herald

SIGNE WILKINSON
Courtesy Philadelphia Daily News

ALAN VITELLO
Courtesy Daily Times-Call (Colo.)

JERRY LEFLER
Courtesy Ventura County Star-Free Press

MIKE KEEFE
Courtesy Denver Post

GEORGE DANBY
Courtesy Bangor Daily News

LINDA BOILEAU
Courtesy Frankfort State Journal

JOHN SHERFFIUS
Courtesy Ventura Star-Free Press

Canada

In September, the election to power of the separatist Parti Quebecois in Quebec was accepted calmly by the rest of Canada. But the stress on a unified Canada increased as Quebec edged toward total separation.

Prime Minister Chrétien visited China on a trade mission, marking the first high-profile trip to that country since the infamous Tiananmen Square massacre, but he scarcely mentioned the issue of human rights.

Canadians who have made their livelihood by fishing have had to face up to the fact that a centuries-old way of life has disappeared since the virtual collapse of the Atlantic Canada commercial fishery two years ago. Marine scientists in the Ministry of Fisheries and Oceans have been at a loss to explain the sudden disappearance of fish stocks. Theories range from the effects of global warming to colder water temperatures, an unchecked seal population, and overfishing by foreign interests. A $2 billion compensation package and a major retraining program for fishery workers has not proved to be a successful solution.

ROY PETERSON
Courtesy Vancouver Sun

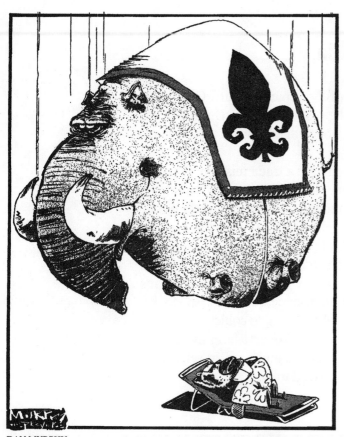

DAN MURPHY
Courtesy Vancouver Province

STEVE NEASE
Courtesy Ottawa Citizen

JOSH BEUTEL
Courtesy Montreal Gazette and Evening Telegraph

STEVE NEASE
Courtesy Ottawa Citizen

EDD ULUSCHAK
Courtesy The Sounder

JAMES GRASDAL
Courtesy Edmonton Journal

"JUST A DARNED MINUTE!"

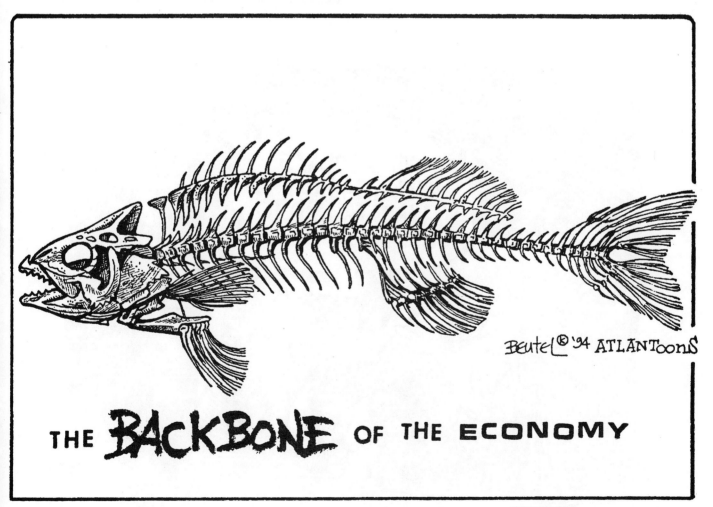

JOSH BEUTEL
Courtesy Montreal Gazette and Evening Telegraph

"SEE HERE, IS THAT GUN REGISTERED?"

Sports

In 1994, for the first time in eighty-four years, there was no baseball World Series. A player strike that began in August ended the season fifty-two days early. Money and power were at the root of the strike, and some long-suffering fans blamed the players while others saw team owners as the main culprits. Players earn an average of $1.2 million a year, and owners have demanded a cap on salaries. Baseball franchises, on the other hand, are increasing in value some 15 percent a year, primarily because of escalating television revenues, and the players contend that teams can afford ever-higher salaries.

A bizarre story unfolded in the normally sedate world of ice figure skating. While preparing for the 1994 Winter Olympics, skating star Nancy Kerrigan was struck on the knee by a hired hoodlum in an effort to keep her out of competition. One of Kerrigan's principal rivals, Tonya Harding, allegedly knew of the attack in advance but told no one. Kerrigan recovered and went on to win the Olympic silver medal, and Harding was barred from competitive ice skating.

Forty-five-year-old George Foreman knocked out Michael Moorer, twenty-six, to become the oldest heavyweight boxing champion of the world. The rotund Foreman previously had held the championship in the 1970s.

BRUCE BEATTIE
Courtesy Daytona Beach News-Journal
©94 Daytona Beach News-Journal
Copley News Service
BEATTIE

"What, are you nuts?! We're not paying for the casket . . . YOU are!"

KEN CATALINO
Courtesy Anchorage Times
CATALINO

THE LAST HERO WORSHIPPER

KIRK WALTERS
Courtesy Toledo Blade

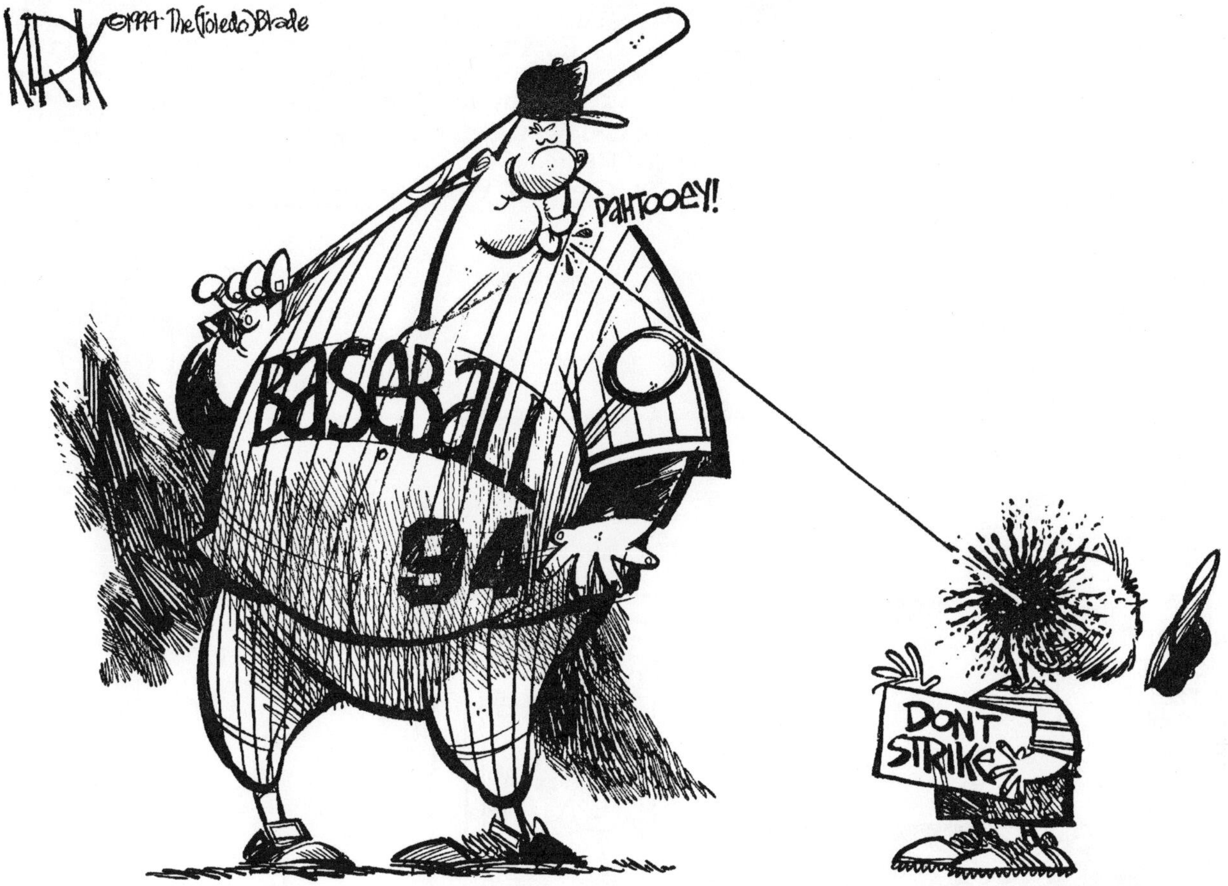
KIRK ©1994 The (Toledo) Blade
PAHTOOEY!
BASEBALL
94
DON'T STRIKE

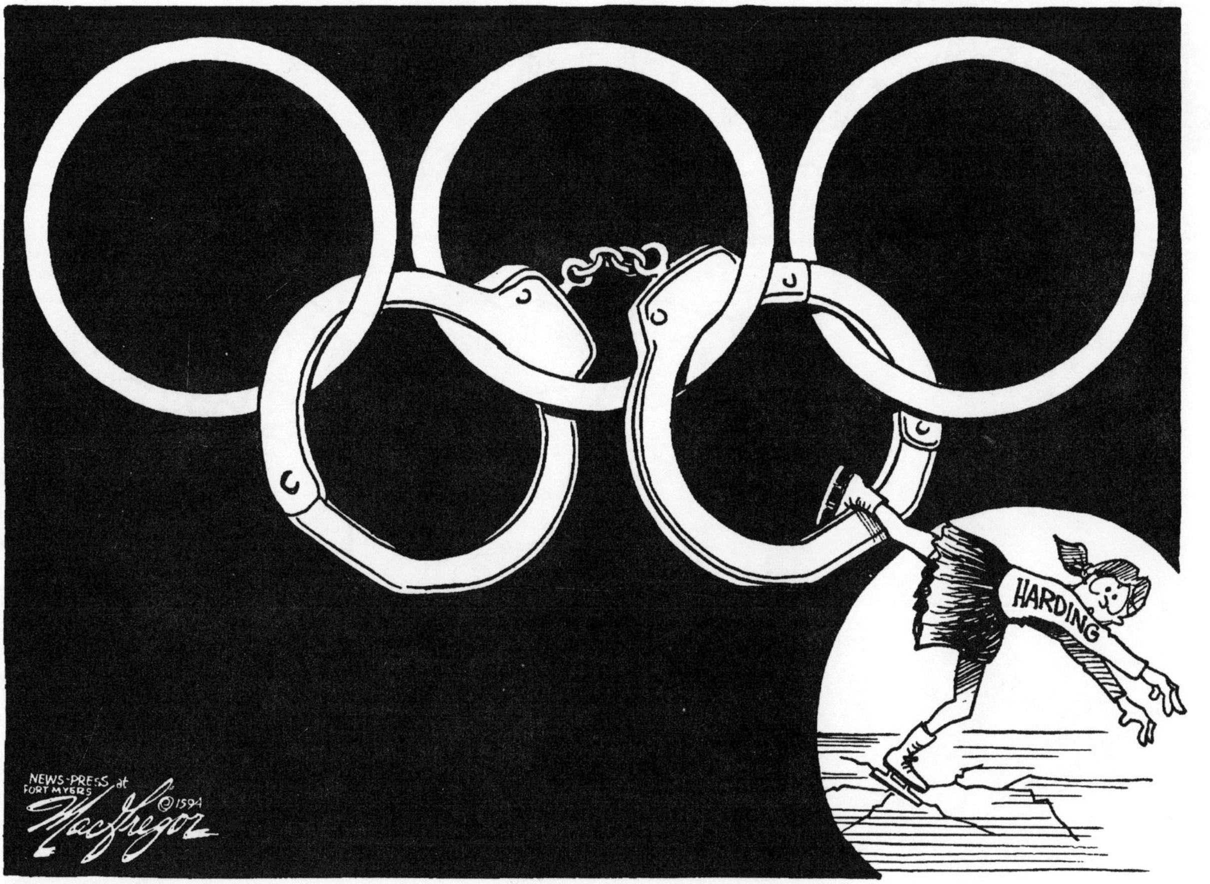
HARDING
NEWS-PRESS at FORT MYERS ©1994 MacGregor

DOUG MACGREGOR
Courtesy Ft. Meyers News-Press

OH, SOMEWHERE IN THIS FAVORED LAND
THE SUN IS SHINING BRIGHT,
THE BAND IS PLAYING SOMEWHERE,
AND SOMEWHERE HEARTS ARE LIGHT;
AND SOMEWHERE MEN ARE LAUGHING,
AND SOMEWHERE CHILDREN SHOUT,
BUT THERE IS NO JOY IN MUDVILLE,
MIGHTY CASEY HAS STRUCK.

"CASEY AT THE BAT." REVISED

CHARLES DANIEL
Courtesy Knoxville News-Sentinel

ED STEIN
Courtesy Rocky Mountain News and NEA

ALAN VITELLO
Courtesy Daily Reporter Herald (Colo.)

176

SCOTT WILLIS
Courtesy San Jose Mercury

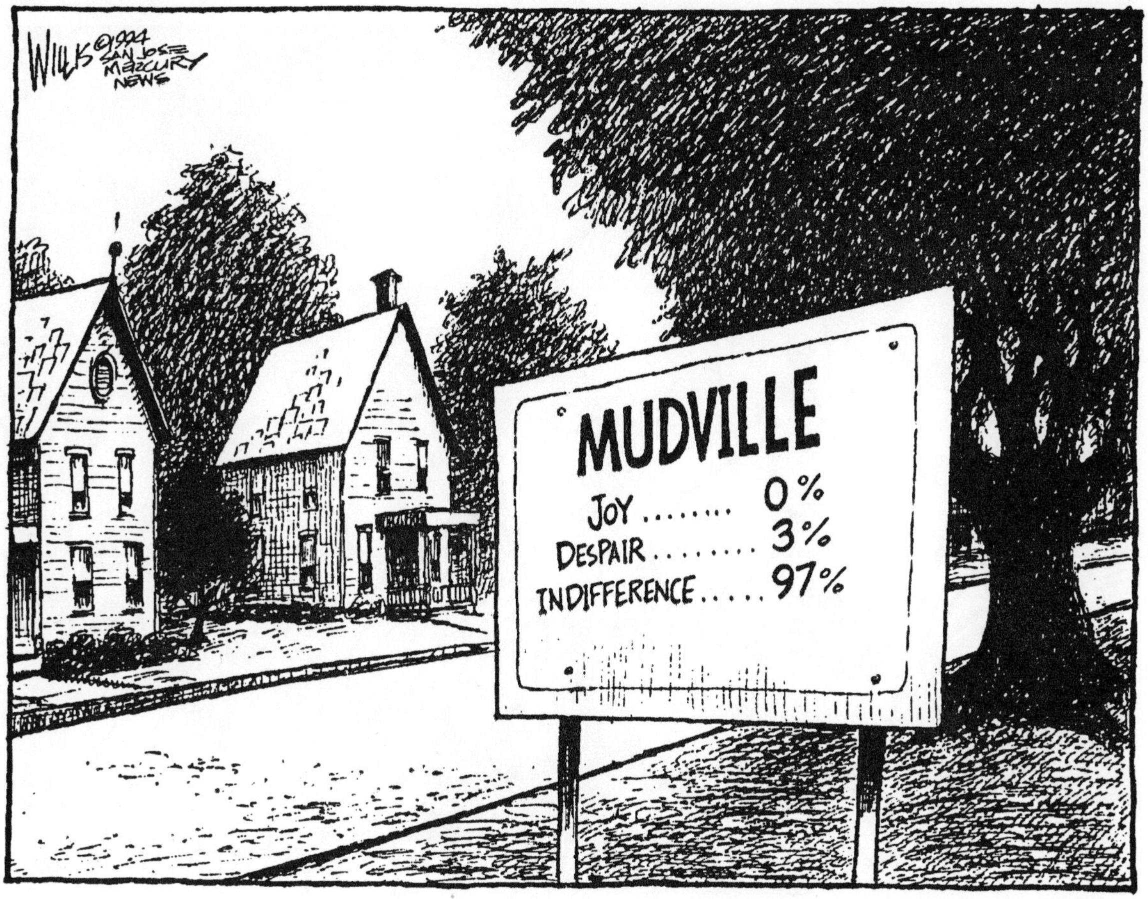
WILLIS ©1994 San Jose Mercury News
MUDVILLE
JOY........ 0%
DESPAIR........ 3%
INDIFFERENCE..... 97%

VIC HARVILLE
Courtesy Arkansas Democrat-Gazette

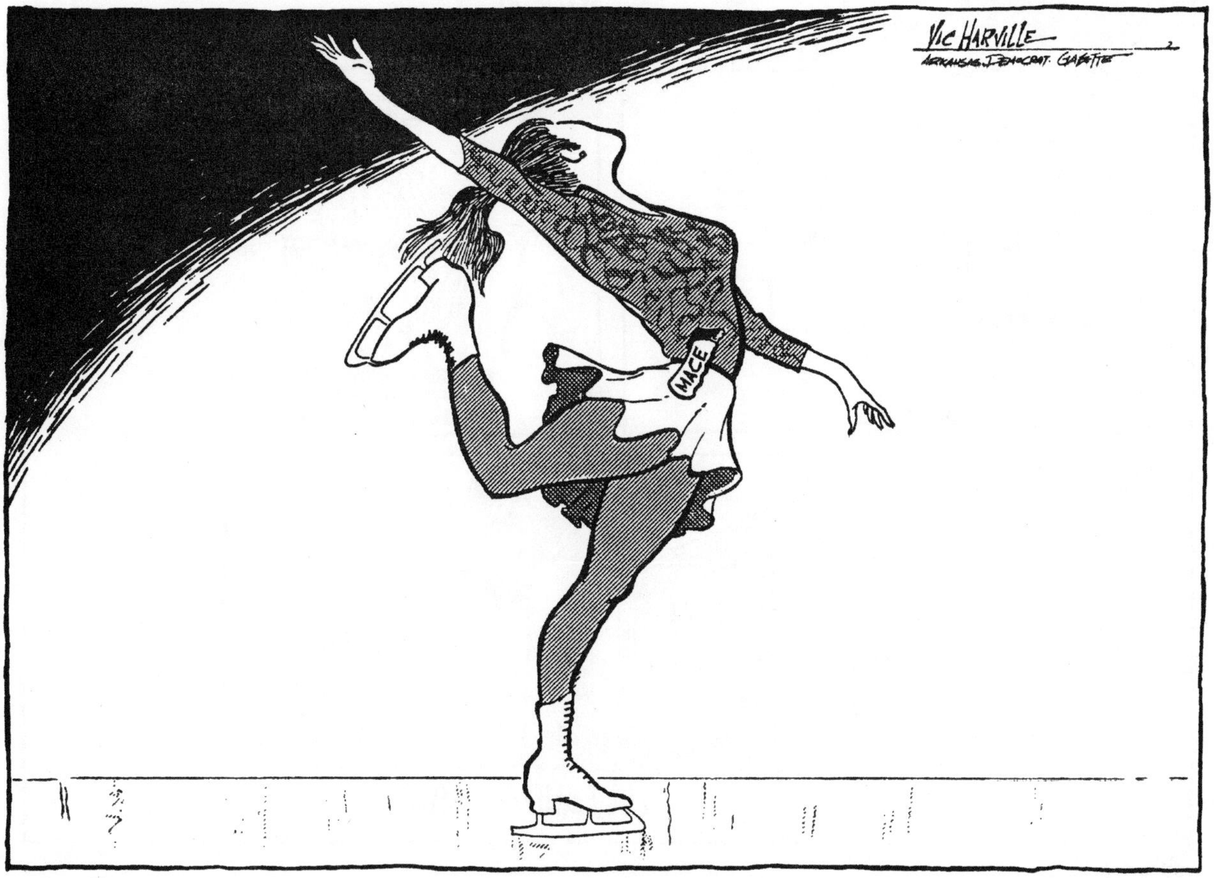
VIC HARVILLE
ARKANSAS DEMOCRAT-GAZETTE
MACE

DAVID HORSEY
Courtesy Seattle Post-Intelligencer

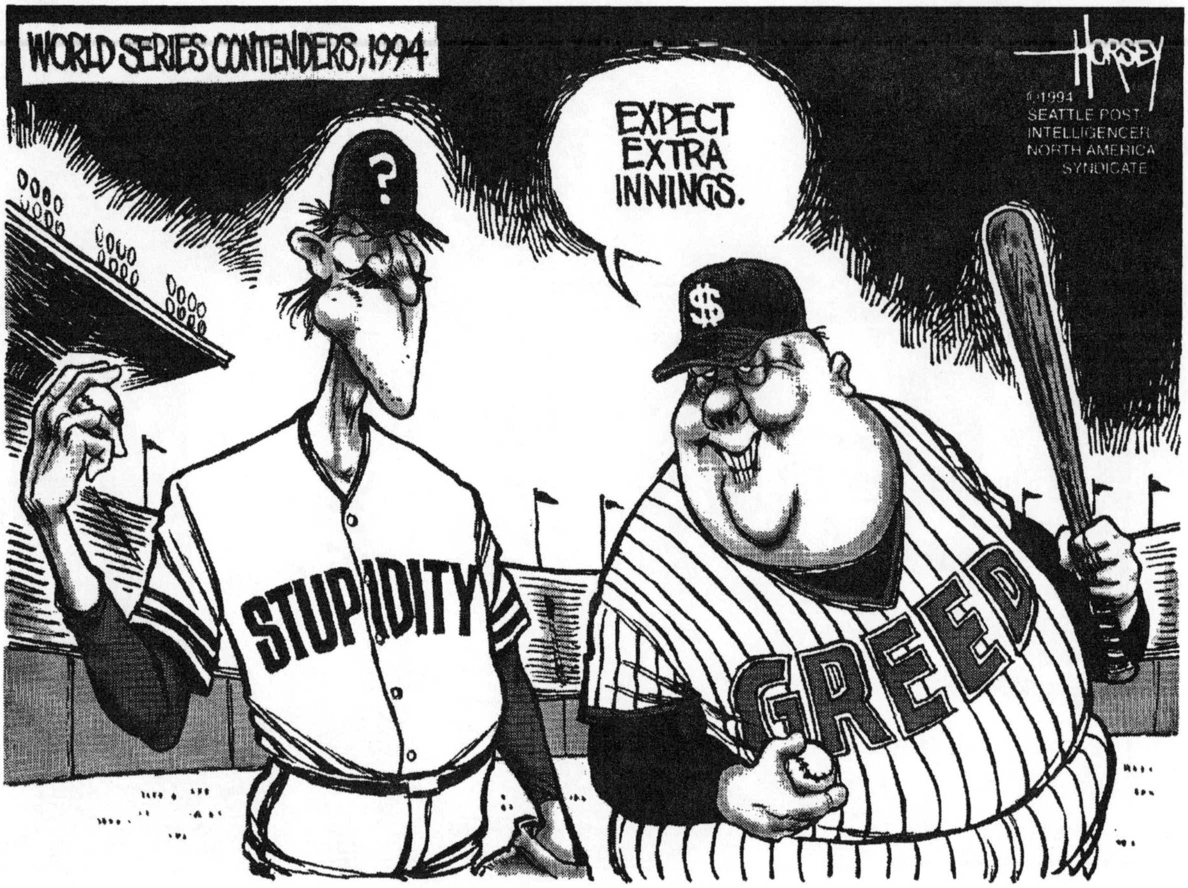
WORLD SERIES CONTENDERS, 1994
HORSEY
©1994 SEATTLE POST-INTELLIGENCER NORTH AMERICA SYNDICATE
EXPECT EXTRA INNINGS.
?
$
STUPIDITY
GREED

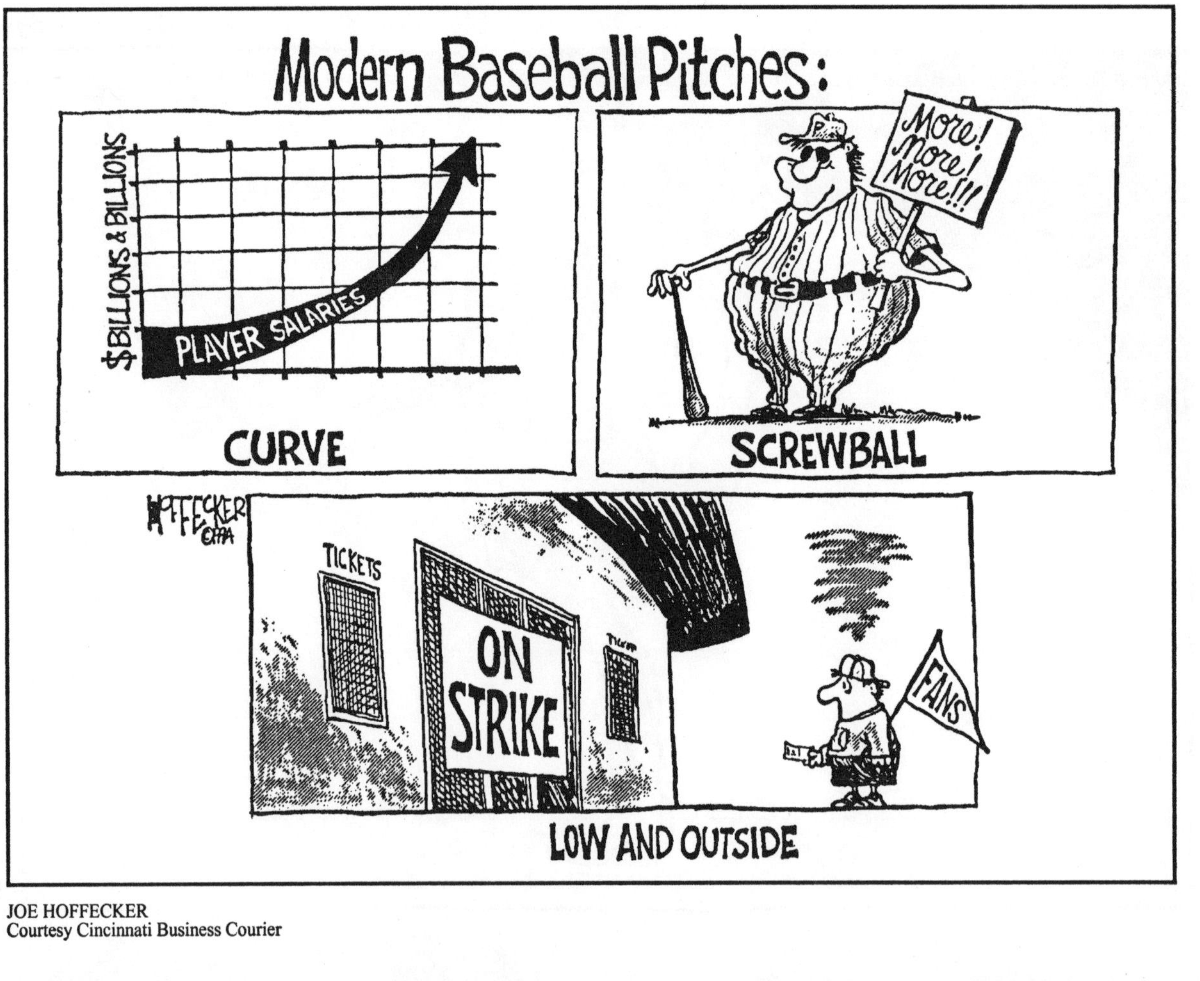
Modern Baseball Pitches:
$ BILLIONS & BILLIONS
PLAYER SALARIES
CURVE
More! More! More!!!
SCREWBALL
HOFFECKER
TICKETS
ON STRIKE
FANS
LOW AND OUTSIDE

JOE HOFFECKER
Courtesy Cincinnati Business Courier

BOB JORGENSEN
Courtesy St. Paul Pioneer-Pess

"A LONG DRAWN OUT STRIKE WOULD BE A REAL DISASTER~ FOUR STAR RESTAURANTS, DOMESTIC CHAMPAGNE, USED FERRARIS..."

MARSHALL RAMSEY
Courtesy Conroe Courier (Tex.)

ERIC SMITH
Courtesy Capital Gazette Newspapers

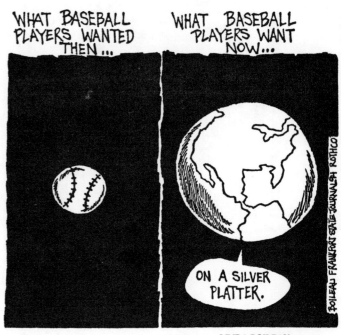

LINDA BOILEAU
Courtesy Frankfort State Journal

CHARLES FAGAN
Courtesy Associated Features Syndicate

STEVE HILL
Courtesy Kansas City Star

Football season kicks off...

San Diego Union-Tribune

MICHAEL CAVNA
Courtesy San Diego Union-Tribune

DON LANDGREN, JR.
Courtesy Clinton Daily Item (Mass.)

T.HARDING —USA
UNSPORTSMANSHIP 6.0
GREED   6.0
CONSPIRACY   6.0
STUPIDITY   6.0

Why beggars hate athletes

RANDY BISH
Courtesy Tribune-Review (Pa.)

CHESTER COMMODORE
Courtesy Chicago Defender

...and Other Issues

June 6, 1994, marked the fiftieth anniversary of D-Day, when Allied forces landed on the beaches of Normandy in the final push to free Europe of Nazi domination and end World War II. A large-scale celebration was held on the beaches to honor both dead and living veterans.

Los Angeles was rocked by a severe earthquake, and later in the year fires and floods further ravaged the state. The White House became the target of would-be assassins. First, a pilot crashed his small airplane into a tree on the White House grounds a few yards from the president's office. Then an intruder was arrested for spraying the White House with a semiautomatic rifle.

The Disney Company abandoned plans for a giant theme park in a historic area of Virginia in the face of strong public opposition. A jury in Albuquerque awarded $2.9 million in damages, later reduced to $640,000, to a woman who sued McDonald's after she spilled a cup of hot coffee in her lap. Oliver North lost a bid for the Virginia Senate seat held by Charles Robb. A book, *The Bell Curve*, which argued that the intelligence level of black Americans is lower than that of Caucasians, sparked a heated controversy.

Celebrities who died in 1994 included Richard Nixon, Jacqueline Kennedy Onassis, and Burt Lancaster.

KIRK WALTERS
Courtesy Toledo Blade

MIKE RITTER
Courtesy Tribune Newspapers

ROB ROGERS
Courtesy Pittsburgh Post-Gazette

BEN SARGENT
Courtesy Austin American Statesman

BILL GARNER
Courtesy Washington Times

185

DENNY PRITCHARD
Courtesy Ottawa Citizen

MERLE R. TINGLEY
Courtesy Toronto Sun

ANN CLEAVES
Courtesy La Prensa (San Diego

Wilma Rudolph (1940–1994)

MICHAEL CAVNA
Courtesy San Diego Union-Tribune

THROUGH AN UNFORTUNATE TWIST OF FATE, 'FAR SIDE' CARTOONIST GARY LARSON FOUND HIMSELF REGISTERED AT THE RETIREMENT HOME FOR CARTOON DRAWINGS, NOT CARTOON DRAWERS.

RICHARD CROWSON
Courtesy Wichita Eagle

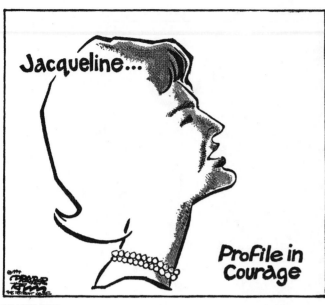

DRAPER HILL
Courtesy Detroit News

DICK WALLMEYER
Courtesy Long Beach Press-Telegram

CHIP BOK
Courtesy Akron Beacon Journal

GLENN MCCOY
Courtesy Belleville News-Democrat (Ill.)

JIM MCCLOSKEY
Courtesy Staunton Daily News Leader

JOEL PETT
Courtesy Lexington Herald-Leader

VIC CANTONE
Courtesy Rothco

MIKE PETERS
Courtesy Dayton Daily News

JACK OHMAN
Courtesy Portland Oregonian

BUT WHAT ABOUT **MY** RIGHTS?

DAN MURPHY
Courtesy Vancouver Province

1913-1994

HERE RESTS IN
HONORED PRIVACY
AN AMERICAN
PRESIDENT
KNOWN BUT TO GOD

DRAPER HILL
Courtesy Detroit News

JIM BORGMAN
Courtesy Cincinnati Enquirer

GOOD DICK

BAD DICK

TRANSCRIPT

"CANCEL MY APPOINTMENTS ..... THIS ONE MAY TAKE AWHILE."

"AS FOR WHITE HOUSE SECURITY, OUR BEST HOPE IS TO PRAY THAT THE NEXT WHACKO WHO FIRES ON THE PLACE ACCIDENTLY SHOOTS DOWN THE NEXT LOONEY WHO TRIES TO CRASH A PLANE THERE."

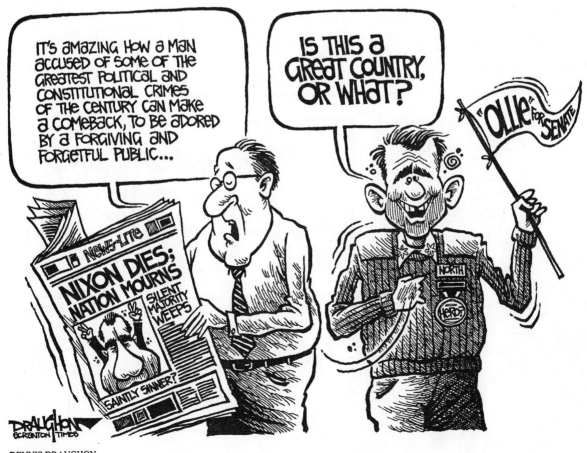

Fill 'Er Up!

ART WOOD
Courtesy Farm Bureau News

JACK MCLEOD
Courtesy Army Times

MIKE PETERS
Courtesy Dayton Daily News

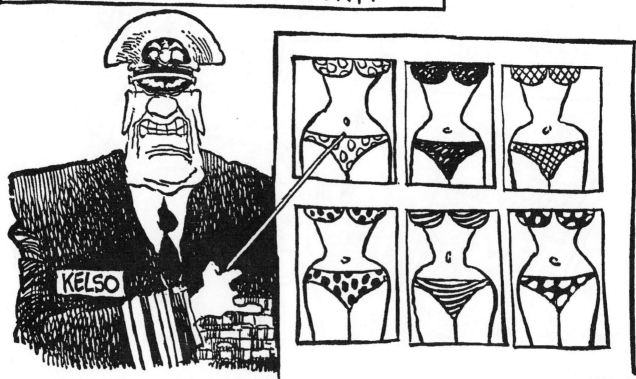

CHIP BOK
Courtesy Akron Beacon Journal

STEVE LINDSTROM
Courtesy Duluth News-Tribune

DAN O'BRIEN
Courtesy Youngstown Daily Business Journal

JEFF KOTERBA
Courtesy Omaha World-Herald

JIM BORGMAN
Courtesy Cincinnati Enquirer

MEANWHILE, ON JUPITER....

BEN SARGENT
Courtesy Austin American Statesman

LARRY WRIGHT
Courtesy Detroit News

DAVID GRANLUND
Courtesy Middlesex News

JERRY BARNETT
Courtesy Indianapolis News

JERRY HOLBERT
Courtesy Boston Herald

TOM DARCY
Courtesy Newsday

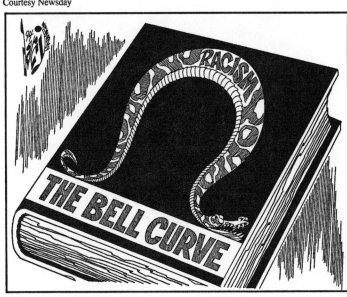

WALT HANDELSMAN
Courtesy Times-Picayune (N.O.)

MIKE LUCKOVICH
Courtesy Atlanta Constitution

CLYDE WELLS
Courtesy Augusta Chronicle

MIKE THOMPSON
Courtesy State Journal-Register (Ill.)

STEVE GREENBERG
Courtesy Seattle Post-Intelligencer

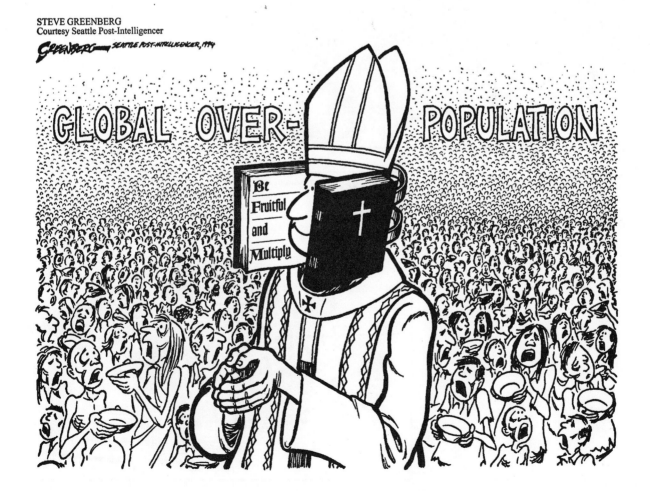

JIMMY MARGULIES
Courtesy The Record (N.J.)/
North American Syndicate

BILL HOGAN
Courtesy Times-Transcript (N. Bruns.)

JIM MCCLOSKEY
Courtesy Staunton Daily News Leader

Past Award Winners

NATIONAL HEADLINERS CLUB AWARD

1938—C. D. Batchelor, New York Daily News
1939—John Knott, Dallas News
1940—Herbert Block, NEA
1941—Charles H. Sykes, Philadelphia Evening Ledger
1942—Jerry Doyle, Philadelphia Record
1943—Vaughn Shoemaker, Chicago Daily News
1944—Roy Justus, Sioux City Journal
1945—F. O. Alexander, Philadelphia Bulletin
1946—Hank Barrow, Associated Press
1947—Cy Hungerford, Pittsburgh Post-Gazette
1948—Tom Little, Nashville Tennessean
1949—Bruce Russell, Los Angeles Times
1950—Dorman Smith, NEA
1951—C. G. Werner, Indianapolis Star
1952—John Fischetti, NEA
1953—James T. Berryman and
        Gib Crocket, Washington Star
1954—Scott Long, Minneapolis Tribune
1955—Leo Thiele, Los Angeles Mirror-News
1956—John Milt Morris, Associated Press
1957—Frank Miller, Des Moines Register
1958—Burris Jenkins, Jr., New York Journal-American
1959—Karl Hubenthal, Los Angeles Examiner
1960—Don Hesse, St. Louis Globe-Democrat
1961—L. D. Warren, Cincinnati Enquirer
1962—Franklin Morse, Los Angeles Mirror
1963—Charles Bissell, Nashville Tennessean
1964—Lou Grant, Oakland Tribune
1965—Merle R. Tingley, London (Ont.) Free Press
1966—Hugh Haynie, Louisville Courier-Journal
1967—Jim Berry, NEA
1968—Warren King, New York News
1969—Larry Barton, Toledo Blade
1970—Bill Crawford, NEA
1971—Ray Osrin, Cleveland Plain Dealer
1972—Jacob Burck, Chicago Sun-Times
1973—Ranan Lurie, New York Times
1974—Tom Darcy, Newsday
1975—Bill Sanders, Milwaukee Journal
1976—No award given
1977—Paul Szep, Boston Globe
1978—Dwane Powell, Raleigh News and Observer
1979—Pat Oliphant, Washington Star
1980—Don Wright, Miami News
1981—Bill Garner, Memphis Commercial Appeal
1982—Mike Peters, Dayton Daily News
1983—Doug Marlette, Charlotte Observer
1984—Steve Benson, Arizona Republic
1985—Bill Day, Detroit Free Press
1986—Mike Keefe, Denver Post
1987—Mike Peters, Dayton Daily News
1988—Doug Marlette, Charlotte Observer
1989—Walt Handelsman, Scranton Times
1990—Robert Ariail, The State
1991—Jim Borgman, Cincinnati Enquirer
1992—Mike Luckovich, Atlanta Constitution
1993—Walt Handelsman, New Orleans Times-Picayune
1994—Mike Peters, Dayton Daily News

PULITZER PRIZE

1922—Rollin Kirby, New York World
1923—No award given
1924—J. N. Darling, New York Herald Tribune
1925—Rollin Kirby, New York World
1926—D. R. Fitzpatrick, St. Louis Post-Dispatch
1927—Nelson Harding, Brooklyn Eagle
1928—Nelson Harding, Brooklyn Eagle
1929—Rollin Kirby, New York World
1930—Charles Macauley, Brooklyn Eagle
1931—Edmund Duffy, Baltimore Sun
1932—John T. McCutcheon, Chicago Tribune
1933—H. M. Talburt, Washington Daily News
1934—Edmund Duffy, Baltimore Sun
1935—Ross A. Lewis, Milwaukee Journal
1936—No award given
1937—C. D. Batchelor, New York Daily News
1938—Vaughn Shoemaker, Chicago Daily News
1939—Charles G. Werner, Daily Oklahoman
1940—Edmund Duffy, Baltimore Sun
1941—Jacob Burck, Chicago Times
1942—Herbert L. Block, NEA
1943—Jay N. Darling, New York Herald Tribune
1944—Clifford K. Berryman, Washington Star
1945—Bill Mauldin, United Features Syndicate
1946—Bruce Russell, Los Angeles Times
1947—Vaughn Shoemaker, Chicago Daily News
1948—Reuben L. ("Rube") Goldberg, New York Sun
1949—Lute Pease, Newark Evening News
1950—James T. Berryman, Washington Star
1951—Reginald W. Manning, Arizona Republic
1952—Fred L. Packer, New York Mirror
1953—Edward D. Kuekes, Cleveland Plain Dealer
1954—Herbert L. Block, Washington Post
1955—Daniel R. Fitzpatrick, St. Louis Post-Dispatch
1956—Robert York, Louisville Times
1957—Tom Little, Nashville Tennessean
1958—Bruce M. Shanks, Buffalo Evening News
1959—Bill Mauldin, St. Louis Post-Dispatch
1960—No award given
1961—Carey Orr, Chicago Tribune
1962—Edmund S. Valtman, Hartford Times
1963—Frank Miller, Des Moines Register

1964—Paul Conrad, Denver Post
1965—No award given
1966—Don Wright, Miami News
1967—Patrick B. Oliphant, Denver Post
1968—Eugene Gray Payne, Charlotte Observer
1969—John Fischetti, Chicago Daily News
1970—Thomas F. Darcy, Newsday
1971—Paul Conrad, Los Angeles Times
1972—Jeffrey K. MacNelly, Richmond News Leader
1973—No award given
1974—Paul Szep, Boston Globe
1975—Garry Trudeau, Universal Press Syndicate
1976—Tony Auth, Philadelphia Enquirer
1977—Paul Szep, Boston Globe
1978—Jeff MacNelly, Richmond News Leader
1979—Herbert Block, Washington Post
1980—Don Wright, Miami News
1981—Mike Peters, Dayton Daily News
1982—Ben Sargent, Austin American-Statesman
1983—Dick Locher, Chicago Tribune
1984—Paul Conrad, Los Angeles Times
1985—Jeff MacNelly, Chicago Tribune
1986—Jules Feiffer, Universal Press Syndicate
1987—Berke Breathed, Washington Post Writers Group
1988—Doug Marlette, Atlanta Constitution
1989—Jack Higgins, Chicago Sun-Times
1990—Tom Toles, Buffalo News
1991—Jim Borgman, Cincinnati Enquirer
1992—Signe Wilkinson, Philadelphia Daily News
1993—Steve Benson, Arizona Republic
1994—Michael Ramirez, Memphis Commercial Appeal

1962—Duncan Macpherson, Toronto Star
1963—Jan Kamienski, Winnipeg Tribune
1964—Ed McNally, Montreal Star
1965—Duncan Macpherson, Toronto Star
1966—Robert W. Chambers, Halifax Chronicle-Herald
1967—Raoul Hunter, Le Soleil, Quebec
1968—Roy Peterson, Vancouver Sun
1969—Edward Uluschak, Edmonton Journal
1970—Duncan Macpherson, Toronto Daily Star
1971—Yardley Jones, Toronto Star
1972—Duncan Macpherson, Toronto Star
1973—John Collins, Montreal Gazette
1974—Blaine, Hamilton Spectator
1975—Roy Peterson, Vancouver Sun
1976—Andy Donato, Toronto Sun
1977—Terry Mosher, Montreal Gazette
1978—Terry Mosher, Montreal Gazette
1979—Edd Uluschak, Edmonton Journal
1980—Vic Roschkov, Toronto Star
1981—Tom Innes, Calgary Herald
1982—Blaine, Hamilton Spectator
1983—Dale Cummings, Winnipeg Free Press
1984—Roy Peterson, Vancouver Sun
1985—Ed Franklin, Toronto Globe and Mail
1986—Brian Gable, Regina Leader Post
1987—Raffi Anderian, Ottawa Citizen
1988—Vance Rodewalt, Calgary Herald
1989—Cameron Cardow, Regina Leader-Post
1990—Roy Peterson, Vancouver Sun
1991—Guy Badeaux, Le Droit, Ottawa
1992—Bruce Mackinnon, Halifax Herald
1993—Bruce Mackinnon, Halifax Herald

NATIONAL NEWSPAPER AWARD / CANADA

1949—Jack Boothe, Toronto Globe and Mail
1950—James G. Reidford, Montreal Star
1951—Len Norris, Vancouver Sun
1952—Robert La Palme, Le Devoir, Montreal
1953—Robert W. Chambers, Halifax Chronicle-Herald
1954—John Collins, Montreal Gazette
1955—Merle R. Tingley, London Free Press
1956—James G. Reidford, Toronto Globe and Mail
1957—James G. Reidford, Toronto Globe and Mail
1958—Raoul Hunter, Le Soleil, Quebec
1959—Duncan Macpherson, Toronto Star
1960—Duncan Macpherson, Toronto Star
1961—Ed McNally, Montreal Star

FISCHETTI AWARD

1982—Lee Judge, Kansas City Times
1983—Bill DeOre, Dallas Morning News
1984—Tom Toles, Buffalo News
1985—Scott Willis, Dallas Times-Herald
1986—Doug Marlette, Charlotte Observer
1987—Dick Locher, Chicago Tribune
1988—Arthur Bok, Akron Beacon-Journal
1989—Lambert Der, Greenville News
1990—Jeff Stahler, Cincinnati Post
1991—Mike Keefe, Denver Post
1992—Doug Marlette, New York Newsday
1993—Bill Schorr, Kansas City Star
1994—John Deering, Arkansas Democrat-Gazette

Index of Cartoonists

INDEX OF CARTOONISTS

COMPLETE YOUR CARTOON COLLECTION

BEST EDITORIAL CARTOONS OF THE YEAR
1995 EDITION
Edited by CHARLES BROOKS

Previous editions of this timeless series are available for those wishing to update their collection of the most provocative moments of the past twenty years. In the early days the topics were the oil crisis, Richard Nixon's presidency, Watergate, and the Vietnam War. Over time the cartoonists and their subjects have changed along with presidential administrations. These days those subjects have been replaced by the Clinton Health Care Reform Bill, the Crime Bill, the NAFTA treaty results, the O. J. Simpson murder trial, and the United States' involvement in Haiti. But in the end, the wit and wisdom of the editorial cartoonists have prevailed. And on the pages of these op-ed galleries one can find memories and much more.

BEST EDITORIAL CARTOONS OF THE YEAR
1994 EDITION
Edited by CHARLES BROOKS

Select from the following supply of past editions

_____ 1972 Edition $18.95 hc	_____ 1982 Edition $14.95 pb	_____ 1991 Edition $14.95 pb
_____ 1974 Edition $18.95 hc	1983 Edition out of print	_____ 1992 Edition $14.95 pb
_____ 1975 Edition $18.95 hc	_____ 1984 Edition $14.95 pb	_____ 1993 Edition $14.95 pb
_____ 1976 Edition $18.95 hc	_____ 1985 Edition $14.95 pb	_____ 1994 Edition $14.95 pb
_____ 1977 Edition $18.95 hc	_____ 1986 Edition $14.95 pb	_____ 1995 Edition $14.95 pb
1978 Edition out of print	_____ 1987 Edition $14.95 pb	
1979 Edition out of print	_____ 1988 Edition $14.95 pb	_____ Please add me to the list
_____ 1980 Edition $18.95 hc	1989 Edition out of print	of standing orders for
_____ 1981 Edition $14.95 pb	_____ 1990 Edition $14.95 pb	future editions.

Please include $2.00 for 4th Class Postage and handling or $3.25 for UPS Ground Shipment plus $.75 for each additional copy ordered.*

Total enclosed: _____

NAME _____

ADDRESS_____

CITY _____ STATE _____ ZIP_____

BEST EDITORIAL CARTOONS OF THE YEAR
1993 EDITION
Edited by CHARLES BROOKS

Make checks payable to

PELICAN PUBLISHING COMPANY
P.O. Box 3110, Dept. 5BEC
Gretna, Louisiana 70054
CREDIT CARD ORDERS CALL 1-800-843-1724

* Jefferson Parish residents add 8¾% tax. All other Louisiana residents add 4% tax.